SPIRITS ONYMOUS

The InnerGuidance Network Handbook 2008

This book is the property of:

_____

When found, please call:

_____

SPIRITS ONYMOUS

The InnerGuidance Network Handbook 2008

**Twelve Principles
for Creating a Magnificent Life**

Practical Steps to Awaken Your Divine Consciousness

Adrianus

IGN
An InnerGuidance Network Publication

DESCRIPTION

This handbook of *The InnerGuidance Network* gives the answer to the most fundamental desire of all human beings. It gives clarity to your spiritual mission and how to create a fulfilling, joyful and abundant existence. In 12 practical steps, in 12 weeks, you can transform your life. You are invited to a supportive community of kindred spirits, raise your energy and create magnificence. The accompanying on-line course is FREE.

Spirits Onymous Handbook 2008 gives easy steps to remember what you came here to do and claim the life you were born to live. This book is for conscious spiritual beings with a passion to create an extraordinary human experience.

If you want love, health, abundance and a meaningful life: this is the book for you. It is a practical tool to focus and attract what you deeply desire.

Spirits Onymous is a book that will help you live and create from a conscious state of mind; aware of who you truly are, aware of your mission and aware of your infinite power. I am Spirit, You are Spirit, All is Spirit, and All is Well.

Additionally, the handbook gives directions to host and facilitate local Spirits Onymous meetings.

Published by IGN
The InnerGuidance Network
PO Box 224, Bethlehem, PA 18016-0224, USA
www.InnerGuidanceNetwork.org

Spirits Onymous Handbook 2008
SECOND EDITION
November 2007

ISBN: 978-0-6151-6446-5
perfect-bound

1. Spirituality, 2. Self Help

COPYRIGHT ALERT

Dedicated to all who are committed
to seeing greatness in self and others.

FOREWORD

I became inspired to write *Spirits Onymous* while I was working on the novel *The ClearView Conspiracy*. John, the main character, meets Moses, an extraordinary spiritual teacher and leader of The InnerGuidance Network. Moses is a man who overcame the limitations of the human mind and sees the world for what it is: a complex energy field in which sparks of Spirit interact with one another.

Moses represents the spiritual wisdom I have gained from countless teachers throughout my life. I feel privileged that I always had the awareness—not the belief, but the knowing—that I am part of a larger entity. Born in a Roman Catholic family, I knew that I was a child of God and born into the world to do something magnificent. As a ten-year-old boy, I didn't know what that was, but I was certain that the world was created for me to interact with. Now I know that everyone is born into this world with the Divine task to manifest a joyful and glorious existence.

From this unwavering place of knowing, I have written twelve steps that will assist you in taking control of the fundamental dynamics of life in such a way that you will no longer be a lost vessel in a rough ocean of drama. The twelve principles provide the formula to calm the waters and create the life you were born to live. After all, you are a very powerful creator!

Many brilliant and insightful books have been written in the past and they may have entertained or even inspired readers for a weekend or possibly a week or two. But, there is a fundamental difference between knowing the truth and living the truth. Hence, *Spirits Onymous* is intended to be more than a book. As the heart of The InnerGuidance Network, *Spirits Onymous* provides an ongoing format for support and education, encouraging you to implement the principles in your life, day-by-day, moment-by-moment.

Why did I choose the name Spirits Onymous? Well, it indicates how we express our true identity in the world. Instead of being anonymous about it, we proudly announce who we are. We are Spirit on a human mission. I am Spirit, You are Spirit, All is Spirit and All is Well.

Adrianus

ACKNOWLEDGEMENTS

I would like to express my gratitude to the wonderful people who participated in the first series of Spirits Onymous meetings in Catasauqua, Pennsylvania: Bill, Casey, Daniel, Heather, Joe, Kathy, Kit, Melissa, Michael, Miriam, Nancy, Patti, Regina, Sharon, Sophia and Zulma. While we kept on tweaking the format, the feedback from these extraordinary spirits helped us test and develop the meeting structure. You may recognize some of the above names later on in the book under testimonials and submitted comments.

Many thanks to the extraordinary people from around the world, who participate in the on-line course. InnerGuidance Network members from Australia, Canada, England, India, Japan, Seychelles, USA, and many more countries, provide an ongoing source of inspiration and encouragement. Thank you!

I would like to extend my profound gratefulness to my "literary team," who lavished me with grammatical suggestions, pointed out ambiguous sections and recommended formatting changes. I want to thank Miriam Dynan, Laurel Leland, Terri Trigiani and Zulma Alvarez.

A special thank you goes to Patricia Omoqui, who elevated the beauty of this book with fourteen of her exquisite poetic meditations. And I am elated that Karen Drucker contributed to the guided meditation/readings that accompany this course. She opens and sets the tone with her heart touching "Blessing to the World."

But first and foremost, I want to thank YOU. I am honored and excited knowing that you have picked up this book. I feel privileged that you have joined me on this incredible journey. I deeply appreciate your company.

TABLE OF CONTENTS

Chapter 1

THE THOUGHT
AND THE PASSION

The soul of the InnerGuidance Network

Can you see Spirit in the eyes of a child?

Thank you for following your heart and reading this book. It will confirm what you already know and invite you to wander into places that you may have forgotten. This book is a tribute to the essence of your being and the magnificence of your journey. You are a spiritual being having a human experience—and what an experience it is! You have been given the opportunity to revel in joy, abundance and divine sweetness.

I discussed this paragraph with my good friend, Adam. "Well," he said after a long silence, "I don't know. When I look around and watch the television, I don't see a lot of happiness. What are we doing wrong?"

We are not doing anything wrong. It is not helpful to resist the present situation, fight it, or blame yourself or others. What is, *is*. However, we can wake up, align with our omnipotent Self, stop the struggle, and focus on what we want to manifest. We are powerful beyond our wildest imagination.

You and I are masterful creators. Look around and recognize that you and your circumstances are products of your own creation. You have manifested every feature of your existence. Your life is like a painting and you are the artist. Every brush stroke, every detail, comes from your hand. Or is it possible that you have passed out your brushes and left your canvas to others to complete? This book will help you reclaim your brushes. It invites you to assume your role as affluent creator.

Know that you have the power to manifest a reality that is in harmony with your deepest desires. Imagine a life that embraces everything that you value: love, purpose, health, abundance, happiness, peace. Imagine living in a reality in which you mindfully create the life you were born to live and allow others to do the same. How does that feel?

A fast growing number of people from many different spiritual traditions, nationalities and cultures acknowledge that the light of Spirit (God, Creator, Yahweh, Brahma, Allah, Universe, Shiva) shines in all of us. Indeed, you are Spirit having a human experience, born to create a magnificent existence. That is what you came here to do. And? Is your life magnificent?

You may not have an ideal job, your health may not be up to par, and your relationship may be a lot less loving than you want it to be. You may be struggling to make ends meet and you may not have a clear grip on your life's purpose either. Are you a failure?

Absolutely not! You just may have forgotten what your life is all about: your existence in physical form. This course will help you remember.

Please take a deep breath and become quiet. Chances are that you will connect with your true Self, which is non-physical. Deep inside, you know that you existed long before your parents arranged for their egg and sperm cells to merge. You know too, that you will continue to exist after you have exhaled your last breath. This lifetime is merely a cosmic daytrip. Soon you will return home and be reunited. But make no mistake. You—so much—desired to be here. You looked forward to this glorious human experience.

Before this lifetime, you were fully conscious and floating in a perpetual state of utter bliss. You never had a bad hair day and never got stuck in traffic. You were always in the here and now, wherever and whenever, instantly. Ecstasy was your average state of mind, until one "day," you felt a little twitch, a subtle feeling of restlessness. Your creative juices were making your hands itch. It's one thing to enjoy perfection; it's another—and ever so satisfying—to create it.

However, you had a predicament. In "heaven" it is not a challenge at all to create something. A mere thought is all that is needed to manifest the highest state of bliss. Creation is instantaneous and doesn't require process. Hence, after "decades" of same-old-same-old bliss, you were ready for the plunge. You felt the uncontrollable urge to bring forth another spiritual masterpiece. That was the moment you decided to take on a physical body. And here you are, in the midst of an exhilarating adventure.

Stop for a moment, take a deep breath and recognize that in your heart pulsates the same passion that moved DaVinci and Michelangelo to create their works of art. So grab your brushes and tap into that genius, that invigorating passion.

"But," Adam interrupted when I read the draft version of this chapter to him, "if we only do what we are passionate about, we wouldn't get anything done. I would be sitting on the beach with a rum-and-coke in my hand, right now."

I had to smile. Certainly, sitting on the beach with a rum-and-coke sounds great, but for how long? If we follow our desire to be happy, we certainly may be drawn to indulge in fun activities. That's okay, since we all know that lasting happiness will only occur when we have a sense of accomplishment and meaning as well. So yes, follow your heart, it will always guide you to a life that will feed your soul: a life that is filled with happiness and worth.

We exist in a moment in space and time in which we—as Spirit in human form—tend to forget our mission and amazing powers. We tend to forget that we are here to manifest magnificence and that our hearts bring forth an elixir of passion that leads the way. So, let's remember that we did not take on physical form to struggle. We are here to express our splendor and create a blissful existence.

You may be thinking that a spiritual journey involves a lot of work and is risky. You may be fearful of losing the level of comfort that you have secured. Fear and the worldly drama around you may have convinced you to settle for mediocrity. But take a deep breath and wonder. What happened to your dreams? Are you passionate about what you are doing? Are you a DaVinci who settled for a "color by number print?" I'm so happy that you're not! You are truly a blessing to the world. Please express yourself fully! Follow your heart. You are Spirit and you have an awesome mission to fulfill. It's time that you throw off your disguise.

Let's stop the masquerade. Let's acknowledge our essence and drop our anonymity. We are Spirit, having a human experience: Spirits Onymous!

This book, and the other tools that The InnerGuidance Network offers, will assist you in claiming your rightful position in the world. Spirits Onymous provides the structure that will help you discover what you came here to do and how to access and hone the creative powers you already possess. A magnificent life is yours to have!

Knowing the truth doesn't mean squat

Knowing the truth but not living it, is like dying of thirst with a glass of water in your hand. The Divine truth that the twelve principles of Spirits Onymous offer will only affect your life when you implement them. You cannot just talk the talk; you must walk the walk. It is the only way that you will accomplish what you want to manifest, whether it is health, love or abundance. If you just read this book and subsequently stick it on your shelf, your thirst for a more meaningful life will certainly continue to swell and there is merit in that. However, if you actually want to take charge of your existence and fill it with love, meaning, joy and abundance, you need to *live* the truth. This handbook and planner will help you with that. It will assist you to transform the mundane into a spectacular spiritual experience.

Yet, it is only a potential. It is completely up to you whether this book will just be an interesting read or a life changing experience. Even though the time investment is minimal, you must commit yourself to doing the work. And if you do, your life will transform before your eyes. Are you in?

Good! This book gives a systematic framework to help you integrate a Divine truth: You are an all-powerful creator able to manifest a magnificent life. The time investment is not much more than 15 minutes a day, but you will be asked to observe your life differently *throughout* the day and adjust some of your routines. Are you still in? ... Great! Before asking you to make five simple commitments (A, B, C, D, E), I want to introduce three crucial concepts:

1. Learning is most effective if it is fun, relaxing and/or exciting.

2. The more you can control your mind and focus on what you want, the more powerful you become.

Why don't you close your eyes and hold for 30 seconds an image of something you really would like to manifest: the car of your dreams, your ideal partner, or a vacation in Bali. Completely focus on that picture and imagine yourself being there: driving that car, embracing your ideal partner, or visiting the local market in Bali. Okay, put this book aside and invest 30 seconds in yourself.

How did you do? Did you feel a smile on your face? If you didn't, try again until you smile, ear to ear, and realize that you have done something very powerful. You have raised your vibrational energy and given your life direction.

3. Almost all behaviors will be integrated in your psyche after doing them consistently for 30 days. Neurological pathways will be created and skills and routines will be firmly incorporated. But it doesn't work when it is done with blood, sweat and tears. Fun, remember, it's got to be fun.

Commitment A

Think of something you would like to manifest within three months. Take a deep breath, close your eyes and visualize it. See it in your mind's eye, hear the sounds and feel the joy in your heart. Concentrate on that for 30 seconds. Now, commit to doing this 30-second exercise for 30 days. After the first month, you may want to increase it to 45 seconds, or a minute, or five minutes.

Commitment B

As you may know, many people tend to get de-hydrated, which causes or aggravates a myriad of physical problems. There is an easy remedy, but let's start slowly. Are you willing to commit to drinking *minimally* three tall glasses of water each day?

To make it fun and help me track how much I drink, I purchased a cool looking one quart container (equivalent of two glasses). On most mornings I fill it up with filtered water from my tap, a freshly squeezed lemon, a bit of cayenne pepper, and a little maple syrup. It tastes great. After the first month, you may want to increase your commitment to four tall glasses a day.

Commitment C

Decide to do something you would love to do anyhow. Keep it fun and start slowly. What about a daily five minute walk? Or a five minute nap during your break? Or saying that you love you partner every day. Or…

Now, go to the planner in the back of this book, look for the current month and fill out A, B and C. For instance:

		A= 30 sec vision, B= 3 glasses water, C= 5 min. walk	A	B	C
Mon	1		√	√	√
Tue	2		√	√	

Commitment D

Keep this handbook and planner with you and record your accomplishments. With the beginning of each month, you decide what you are committed to do for that month. You can pick anything, as long as it is **FUN** and take **small steps**. It is not about forcing anything; it is about establishing lasting change **with ease**. You certainly can renew a commitment for another month, or scale back.

Commitment E

Celebrate! Not necessarily with white flour, sugar and fatty dinners, but yes, celebrate your success! Buy a book, get a massage or go on a trip.

Chapter 2

THE INNERGUIDANCE NETWORK

Mission and services

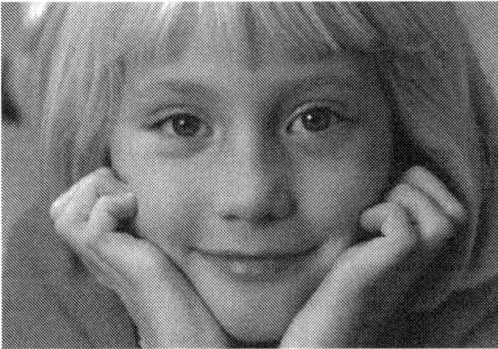

Can you see Spirit, beaming in her eyes?

The foundation of The InnerGuidance Network (IGN) is the awareness that we are spiritual beings having the power of creating glorious human experiences. Life is meant to be purposeful and joyful.

Through the Spirits Onymous program, IGN offers a non-stop educational and supportive structure for anyone who is inspired to recognize greatness in self and others and who wants to create a meaningful and joyful existence—*and allow others to do the same*. The Network is nondenominational and welcomes people from all walks of life.

The InnerGuidance Network offers members support to increase their vibrational energy and together increase the energy around the world, inviting love and peace to prosper, one soul at a time. The educational and supportive structure consists of several elements:

The ClearView Conspiracy
The novel *The ClearView Conspiracy* is a fast-paced spiritual adventure that takes readers on a thought-provoking quest deep into their own soul. *The ClearView Conspiracy* introduces the twelve principles in an exciting package. It is a great introduction for those that are new to Spirits Onymous and it invites the seasoned spiritual traveler to go deeper. But above all, if you like adventure stories, it's great entertainment. For more information: www.ClearViewConspiracy.com.

In order to reach millions worldwide, we anticipate contracting with a reputable and ambitious publisher in the near future. In the meantime, The ClearView Conspiracy is available to the members of The InnerGuidance Network at www.InnerGuidanceNetwork.org: click on "Spirits Onymous," and when you are on campus, click on "Members Store." The book is available as a PDF download and a paperback.

"The ClearView Conspiracy gave me a jump-start to a place within which I really understand that we are all Spirits here to do spiritual work. Layers of forgetting were allowed to drop away, and I find such joy in viewing myself and others in this wonderful light..."
- Barbara, Texas

"I actually found myself falling into childhood behavior of "gorge reading," and needed to stop myself, walk away and commit to slowing the pace. I am very intrigued."
- Melissa, Pennsylvania

"Your book threw me into a tailspin! Thank you for this wonderful book. I read it in one afternoon! I just couldn't put it down."
- Cas, Florida

Spirits Onymous Handbook

This book is created to be an easy reference, planner and a daily companion for InnerGuidance Network members. It gives a synopsis of the twelve steps and provides concrete guidelines to integrate the principles into daily life. Additionally, it gives directions and tools to host and facilitate Spirits Onymous meetings.

Spirits Onymous E-course

The Spirits Onymous course is offered free of charge at the website: www.InnerGuidanceNetwork.org. The on-line campus is frequently updated, offers streaming audio and video programs, guided meditations, message boards and links to related content. Every week, InnerGuidance Network members receive an email with a short text to contemplate and an invitation to read the course material.

Spirits Onymous meetings

Members are encouraged to set up bi-weekly Spirits Onymous meetings. The format is similar to what is provided on the website, with the added value that like-minded people actually meet in person, creating local communities and peer-coaching relationships.

Telephone meetings

Spirits Onymous meetings will be available over the telephone. The structure is the same as the local Spirits Onymous meetings. Check the website for details.

Workshops

The InnerGuidance Network offers a variety of workshops for which continuing education credits are offered. It's best to check the website for CE information, dates and locations. Additionally, we are offering on-line courses. The cornerstone workshops are:

- ❑ The Art of Mindful Creation
- ❑ The Art of Mindful Living: Creating Physical Resilience
- ❑ The Art of Mindful Communication

Certified IGN Coaches

Certified Life Coaches are available to assist members with the process of identifying and manifesting an extraordinary life.

Certified Peer Coaches

Members are invited to create peer-coaching relationships with other members. In order to do this responsibly, all members are strongly encouraged to register for The Art of Mindful Communication workshop. The workshop, which is offered live as well as on-line, teaches the fundamental dynamics of establishing a supportive and empowering peer-coaching relationship.

After completion of this workshop and a 12-week participation in a Spirits Onymous meeting, members will receive a certificate of peer-coaching. If a local meeting is not available, other avenues are offered. Please check the website.

YOU

If you are like most other people, you have made many resolutions in your life, only to see that down the road you were not quite able to stick to your plans. Why was that? Most likely, because it wasn't fun, you lost focus or you lacked support.

Consciously or subconsciously, you have attracted this book into your life because you have a deep desire to create a magnificent and meaningful life. And my friend, you deserve to succeed!

To increase the likelihood that you will transform your life within the next six to twelve months, it's wise to:

1. Go online, register and set aside time to do the course.

2. Join a local Spirits Onymous group, set one up, or invite friends to do the course with you.

3. Get a peer coach when you join a group.

4. Consider hiring a professional life coach.

5. Remember to have fun. The course is meant to be fun. Keep it so!

Chapter 3

THE TWELVE PRINCIPLES

Twelve principles for creating
a purposeful, successful and joy filled life

Look into the eyes of your neighbor
and into your own.
Find it. It's there. Spirit is You.

The Twelve Principles of Spirits Onymous

1. Align with your True Identity

2. Align with Stillness

3. Align with Now

4. Align with your Original Intent

5. Align with your Inner Guide

6. Create a Goal Plan

7. Take Charge: The R-factor

8. Create Mindfully

9. Reach Enlightenment Now

10. Be a Mindful Leader

11. Maintain Physical Resilience

12. Maintain a Sustainable World

Before We Begin

This book is best read over a period of thirteen weeks, in symphony with others and the website. Four times a year, the course is offered in a variety of formats. You can go on-line and join the free E-course at www.InnerGuidanceNetwork.org, seek or start a local Spirits Onymous meeting, call in for a tele-meeting or get support from an InnerGuidance Network coach. Whether you go on-line, call in, or go to a meeting, the same steps will be discussed. The local Spirits Onymous meetings are further discussed in Chapter 4 of this book.

Invite friends and family to do the course with you. You'll make the course immeasurably more powerful when you reach out and share your experience with others, especially with those who are close to you.   But you don't need to put this book aside until you have found a meeting or registered online. By all means, breeze through it, sample it or read the book and do the exercises on your own. I feel honored and excited that you have joined me on this miraculous journey, in any which way that feels good to you.

Before we begin discussing the principles, I would like to introduce you to a powerful method that may dramatically impact the way you experience life. It certainly has mine. It's the number one technique to fight stress, become grounded, and create a sense of well-being.

Do you have any idea what that could be? As a matter of fact, it is so powerful that we will begin every meeting with this technique. On the following page, you will find the answer.

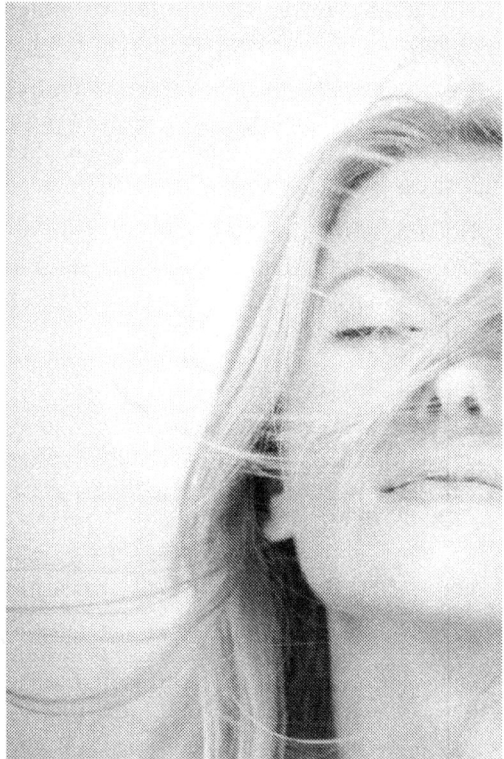

Natural Breathing

Not so long ago, women fainted for just about everything. A mouse, sudden noise, bad news; down they went. People still faint, but clearly a lot less often. Why? Well, when we are startled or frightened our bodies produce adrenaline, which alerts every muscle we have to get ready to fight or to flee. Subsequently, we need more oxygen to "feed" our muscles. In order to accomplish this, we need to breathe in more air. We start to use our lungs more fully and breathe more frequently. Makes sense right?

However, there was a time that women wore corsets—very tight corsets—which only allowed them to breathe very superficially. Result: in times of stress their bodies did not get the oxygen they needed, they became light headed, dizzy--and fainted.

Still, even without corsets, many people do not use the full capacity of their lungs. They breathe shallowly. When they are under stress, they tend to become nervous and panicky—partly due to lack of oxygen. That's why it is so important to breathe the natural way: always breathe from the abdomen and expand the rest of your lungs when you need more oxygen.

Do you breathe the natural way? Well, let's explore. Put your hand on your abdomen; what do you feel? Do you feel movement? What happens when you are stressed? Did you know that mindful breathers can reduce their stress by just changing the way they breathe?

Become a mindful breather and help your body remember the natural way of breathing. This week, claim time to reacquaint yourself with the three movements of Natural Breathing: belly breathing, median chest breathing and shallow breathing.

Practice the four exercises below in bed before going to sleep or before getting up in the morning. Almost everyone breathes from the abdomen in the early morning. Be gentle and only practice for a couple of minutes at a time.

1. Abdominal Breathing or Belly Breathing

▶ Relax the belly muscles and concentrate on your abdomen.

▶ Inhale through the nose, bring the air to your abdomen and feel your belly rise.

▶ Gently tense your belly muscles and breathe out calmly through the mouth.

Continue until you can belly breathe without any effort. Check the movements by putting your hand on your belly, just under your navel.

2. Median Chest Breathing

▶ Inhale by expanding your rib cage

▶ Exhale by contracting your rib cage

Check the movements by softly pressing your hands against the sides of your rib cage. When you expand your rib cage, your stomach muscles may tighten up a little bit. That's okay. Your body might have forgotten what it once was able to do naturally. But with a little training, your body will soon remember.

3. Shallow Breathing

▶ Inhale by raising your sternum (chest bone)

▶ Exhale by lowering your sternum

Check the movements by putting one of your hands on your sternum.

4. Full Breathing

Here, we combine the three breathing movements in a natural rhythm.

▶ Inhale calmly by raising your abdomen, followed by your rib cage, and sternum.

▶ Exhale by calmly lowering your abdomen, followed by contracting your rib cage, and lowering your sternum.

Natural Breathing

The above exercises help you rediscover the movements of Natural Breathing. The main message is that you always breath from your abdomen. When you are truly relaxed, you will notice that your breathing is low: your belly goes up and down, while your chest remains at rest. This is natural. When you need more oxygen you will start using more of your lung capacity by moving your rib cage and sternum as well. All this will happen naturally.

RECLAIMING SPIRIT 1

Do the breathing exercise every day before going to bed, until you have mastered "Natural" or "Full Breathing." Monitor the way you are breathing throughout the day for the rest of the week. Check regularly. How do you breathe during calm moments and stressful moments? Just monitor. When you become aware that your breath is becoming shallow or when you are holding your breath, gently let go and deepen your breathing.

RECLAIMING SPIRIT 2

Whenever you feel that you are becoming tense, check the way you are breathing. Take a deep breath and relax your body. Think of something pleasant and bring your breathing down to your abdomen. This is a very effective way to relax and regain control.

RECLAIMING SPIRIT 3

Invite friends and family to do the course with you.

"I worked with Dr. Bernardo Merizalde and he asked me to do a breathing exercise. I put an empty plastic juice bottle to my abdomen and leaned against the wall. As I breathed into my abdomen I moved back and forth, a physical demonstration of the difference in breathing fully. Now I get to read your exercise... This is definitely the lesson I need to take in. Thank you."

- Kit

"I'm enjoying using the Course to focus and rejuvenate while I muddle through school. I've found that focusing in the NOW allows me a reprieve from the "chatter" and projection. Full time work, full time school make for a very full and over-extended life, so moments of "Being" are vital right now."

- Melissa

As you take a few deep breaths this morning, envision yourself opening up wide so that you can receive the beautiful gifts that are on their way into your life.

Breathe Deeply

Trust

Be calm

Find open space inside for newness to arrive

Relax

Receive

Many gifts are on the way

You are more and more ready for these changes each day

Be proud of yourself for your progress

Celebrate

     Each tiny step forward

     Each small move you make towards your passion

For this takes bravery and courage and guts

You are doing well

Launch your seeds into the Universe

Then

Trust, Relax, Wait

Expect miracles

Rejoice at the big one and small ones

Patricia Omoqui

I am Spirit
You are Spirit
All is Spirit
and
All is Well

Align with your True Identity

**There's only one truth, one reality, and that is Divine Consciousness.
I am Spirit, You are Spirit, All is Spirit.**

—

Sooner or later, everyone wonders: Has my life a purpose? Is there a higher power? Where did I come from? What will happen after I die?

Most human beings have an ego—a sense of Self—that is only a meager representation of the truth. The swan that was born among ducks derived its sense of Self by how the ducks saw him: ugly. Where does your sense of Self come from? How do you identify yourSelf?

You may say, "I'm an accountant, mother of three daughters and a recovering trauma survivor." But is that who you are? Is that the essence of your being? Take a deep breath, close your eyes and strip yourself of all your labels, possessions and character traits. What's left?

The truth of the matter is that you are Spirit. Not just an apprentice Spirit … you are one hundred percent, full-fledged, genuine Spirit. You don't have to do anything to become Spirit … you are Spirit.

We are all part of the same Divine entity (God, Spirit, Allah, Brahman, Cosmos), but like water, not even Spirit can afford to be stagnant. Hence, Spirit (you and I and the rest of us) created earth, as a place in time and space to engage in an *ongoing* process of rejuvenation.

—

We are Spirit, having a human experience. As spiritual beings, we've accepted "physical" form to *joyfully* recreate and redefine our true Self, which is non-physical, which is Divine Consciousness.

Moment of Contemplation

Please get comfortable, close your eyes and let the text sink in. Observe whatever comes up. Don't judge or analyze, just observe. Use the space below to write down your thoughts and insights.

RECLAIMING SPIRIT 1

So, who are you? Take a deep breath and go within. With whom or with what do you identify yourself? When a job title or legal status comes up, be appreciative for that tidbit of information and restate the question, "Who am I?" You may not get a complete answer, maybe just a feeling. Go with that...

RECLAIMING SPIRIT 2

Whenever you can, focus on your breathing and repeat silently, on every inhalation, "I am Spirit," and see what happens.

RECLAIMING SPIRIT 3

Go to chapter 6 and fill out the section of the *Gratitude List* and the *Transformation and Vision List* for this week. Here is where the rubber meets the road. This will help you bring spirituality into the world. Filling out the forms, implementing your intentions and reviewing them weekly will help you transform your life into a phenomenal experience.

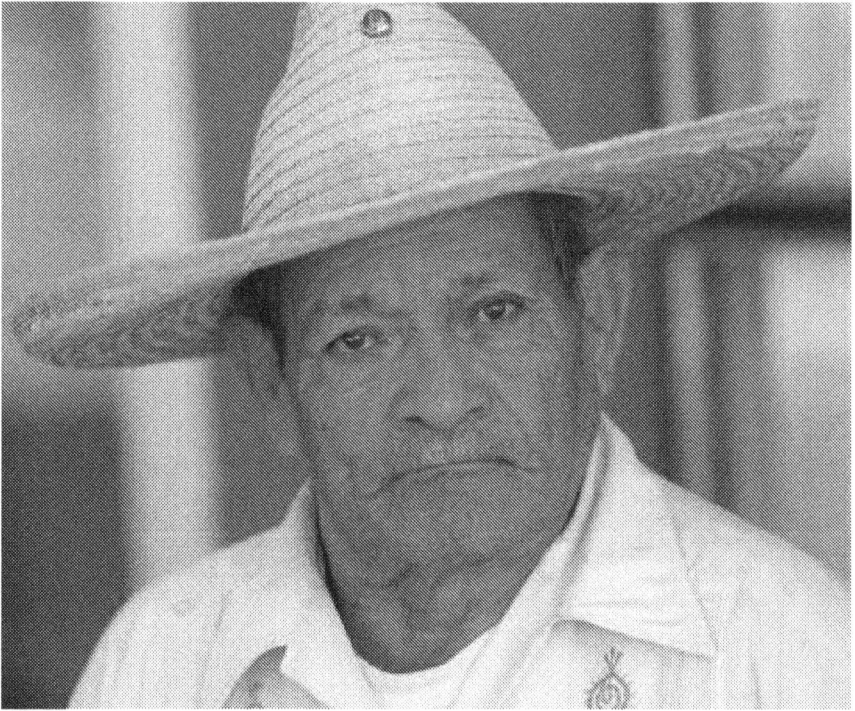

I am Spirit and so are You.

"Step one is a beautiful reminder of being more than our roles or defined labels of ourselves. I like the breathing exercise with the connecting point to spirit. It really connects me to the power within. I will enjoy doing this exercise throughout the week."

- Laurel

"Our Creator was in His creative process...
He created us to be like Him...
Ergo, we are to fulfill the creative process... That's good!"

- William

There is more on campus at www.InnerGuidanceNetwork.org:

❏ Discover what your birthright is

❏ Learn why people put themselves in painful situations

❏ Relax deeply and gain new insights with guided meditations

I am Spirit and so are You.

We are all connected. We are all One. Separation is illusion.

You are learning to see
No distinction in anyone

You are all the same
You are all Source energy

This separation of bodies and spirits
Is simply illusion

You are beginning to experience
The breaking down of the illusion

Only be disillusioned with the illusion
Only be disheartened by not following your truth

Patricia Omoqui

I am Spirit
You are Spirit
All is Spirit
and
All is Well

Step 2

Align with Stillness

In the depth of stillness, you will acquire the full power of the mind and find answers to all life defining questions.

–

As spiritual beings having a human experience, many of us lose focus and get swept away by a tidal wave of drama. Like an over excitable dog, we start chasing our own tail and snapping at everyone who challenges our preconceived notions.

Due to experiences and a socialization process, many of us identify ourselves with only a meager representation of who we truly are. Instead of powerful beings, we tend to see ourselves as failures and seek approval and recognition from others.

Your mind, like a faithful dog, will protect you according to how you relate to the world. If you perceive the world as threatening, your mind will respond likewise. It will be hyper-vigilant and ready to flee, fight or freeze. It will try to control the people and circumstances around you. This is a state of mind that feeds drama and creates wars.

We need to dissolve our attachment to drama and focus the mind on the truth: I am Spirit, You are Spirit, All is Spirit, and All is Well. As spiritual beings, we took on physical form to bring into manifestation the purest forms of consciousness. We are here to create magnificent lives. That's what our minds need to be focused on. The human mind is a powerful tool, but you need to be in charge: Spirit.

–

Meditate and acquire the skills to focus your mind and emerge in stillness. Your life will gain peace and balance. Answers to life defining questions will come to you—with ease.

Moment of Contemplation

Please get comfortable, close your eyes and let the text sink in. Observe the feelings and thoughts that come up. Don't judge or analyze, just observe. Use the space below to write down your thoughts and insights.

∼⚬∼

MEDITATION

I would like to encourage you to experiment with as many forms of meditation that come within your reach. Meditation is the act of concentrating and calming the mind. It is the act of leaving the stressful world behind and going within.

Meditation has several distinctive phases:

▶ First, you need to decide what to focus on during your meditation. You could focus on a text that is deeply anchored in your belief system (prayer, mantra, affirmation), an object (candle, statue), or your breath (the gentle rhythm of your belly going up and down).

▶ Get comfortable, preferably sitting upright with a straight back. Quiet your mind, relax your muscles, close your eyes (optional) and focus your attention on your breath, object or text (prayer, mantra, affirmation) of your choice.

► Breathe calmly from your abdomen and—if you like—repeat your mantra, prayer or affirmation silently to the rhythm of your breath.

► When a thought comes up, do not engage yourself in that thought. Instead, look at the thought as though it were a cloud in the blue sky. Imagine a breeze moving the thought along and refocus on your breath, the text, or the object. Thoughts are to be expected. Just calmly acknowledge that you are thinking about something. Accept that fact. Now, respectfully and with loving care, distance yourself from the thought and refocus on your breath, mantra, or object.

► After some practice you may become free of thought for short moments. The more you practice meditation, the longer you may become "thought-less." This state is very healing for body and mind. Meditation will help develop your skills of focusing your thoughts and fine-tuning your intuitive powers.

► Sometimes, people go into a deep meditative state and experience revelations or acquire spiritual insights.

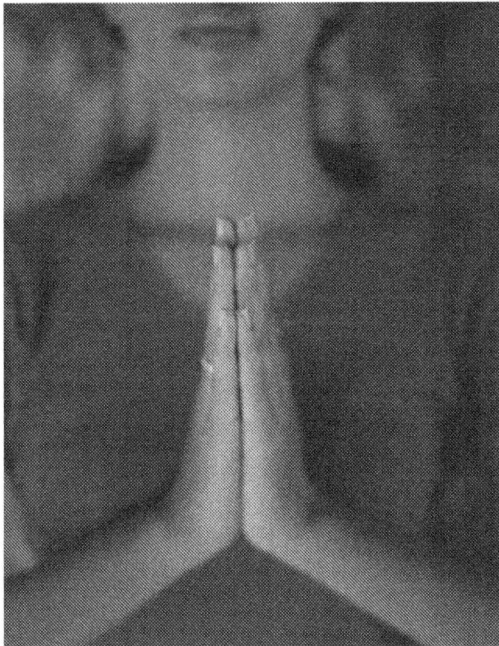

When you acquire the skills to focus your mind and emerge in stillness, your life will gain peace and balance. You will develop mastery of your most powerful instrument for creating the life that you desire—focused thought.

In *The ClearView Conspiracy*, Channary shows us her routine to focus her mind: "[...] and taking a deep breath, [Channary] repositioned herself on the bed, folded her legs, closed her eyes, focused her mind and went into a state of meditation. Her mind slowed down. At first, Channary focused on her breath, not intending to change anything. She just observed her belly going in ... and out... in...and out... As an experienced meditator, she noticed a pleasant shift in her body and became aware of a warm sensation in the palms of her hands. Channary smiled. She breathed deeply and sunk deeper into a state of altered consciousness. Whenever she started to think about something, she noticed this and visualized the thought as a cloud. She invited the cloud to drift by, and refocused on her breathing: in ... and out... in and out... Starting from the top of her head all the way down to her toes, she allowed her muscles to relax. Little by little, her state of mind shifted from being limited to her body to a more limitless consciousness, in which she could access a deeper knowing."

RECLAIMING SPIRIT 1

Create a <u>daily routine</u> of deeply relaxing your body and mind through relaxation and breathing exercises, meditation and/or mindful movement, e.g. Tai Chi, Chi Kung or yoga. It is important that you relax at least twice a day. Ideally, do a short relaxation exercise before you go to work in the morning, after lunch, and when you go to bed. Start out with just a couple of minutes, maybe five.

For the duration of this course, listen to the audio program *Rejuvenation for Body and Mind* while falling asleep. Do this every day. To order, go to the online store at www.InnerGuidanceNetwork.org.

RECLAIMING SPIRIT 2

Meditate once or twice daily. Start out with five minutes. You may want to use a timer. Do not meditate longer than five minutes, unless you repeatedly have the urge to do so. Then, and only then, meditate for ten minutes. This way, you can build up to longer meditation sessions. But if five minutes feels good, great!

RECLAIMING SPIRIT 3

Go to Chapter 6 and fill out the section of the *Gratitude List* and the *Transformation and Vision List* for this week.

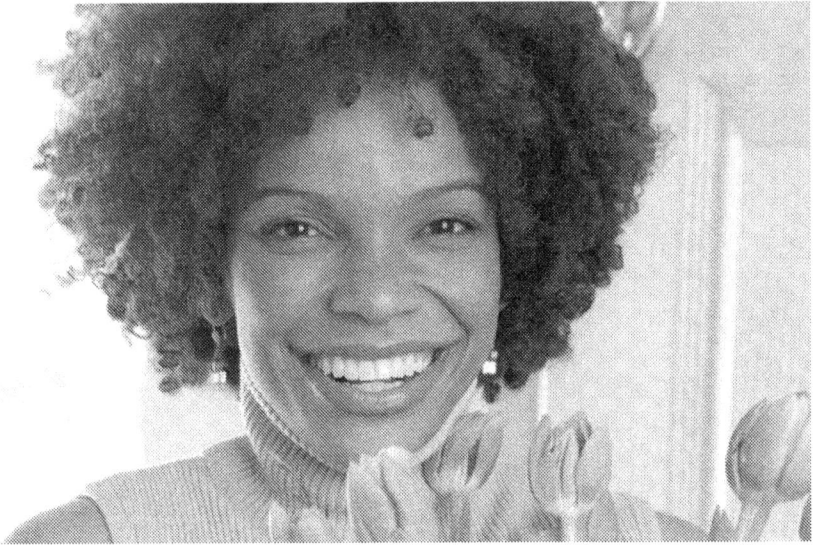

I am Spirit and so are You.

"When I read what you have written I say "of course". "He's right". I know this.... How is it that I forget, get stuck in the negative, time after time???"

- K.

"Being Spirits, it makes it easier to understand that we are all connected, to each other and to all of creation. That concept would be much more difficult without the knowledge we all seek throughout our lives. I feel very fortunate to be able to continue my journey and will always be seeking knowledge, that which has been forgotten, and that which remains unknown."

- Donald

"Stress "is" and we make of it what we will.
The thought occurred to me:
I am not the planter;
I am not the cultivator;
I am the soil."

-William

There is more on campus at www.InnerGuidanceNetwork.org:

- ❑ Learn the five essential steps to reducing stress, anger and fear
- ❑ Learn the skills to become a powerful creator
- ❑ Relax deeply and gain new insights with guided meditations

I am Spirit and so are You.

Find beauty in the quiet times of life.

There is beauty in simply being

Being quietly with yourself

No need to do

Just sitting quietly

Listening to the silence

Feeling the comfort and peace in the silence

Hearing the inspired words come to your soul

Make the Silence your Friend

Silence offers you many gifts

If you forget to spend time in Silence

You neglect your Soul Mate

 A Soul Mate with so much to offer you

Sit

Be Silent

Relax

Breathe Deeply

Breathe Intentionally

Live your life on purpose

By Being

Being

Being

By Being before Doing

Patricia Omoqui

I am Spirit
You are Spirit
All is Spirit
and
All is Well

Align with Now

**True happiness can only be created one moment at a time,
and that moment is always now.**

–

You are invited to synchronize your internal clock to the moment in time where the rest of your life is created: *the Now*. A joyful, meaningful and love-filled existence can only be created one moment at a time, and that moment is *always* now. What "was" is gone and what "will be" has not arrived yet. So, if you want to have a great life, you better grab it before it slips through your fingers.

We came into physical form to engage in a creation process that never ends and always happens in *the Now*. Let's realize this and enjoy the journey!

But are you <u>willing</u> to be amazed, loved, prosperous, healthy and respected? Are you really? Are you truly willing to be happy—at this very moment? Even on Monday mornings or when you are paying your bills? We can only create a happy tomorrow if we celebrate what we have today.

–

The very nature of our existence is not reaching a certain goal, it is the *process*. It is creation itself. We came into physical form to engage in a creation process that never ends and always happens in *the Now*. Let's realize this and enjoy the journey! Life is like a vacation. You want to savor each and every moment.

Moment of Contemplation

Please get comfortable, close your eyes and let the text sink in. Observe the feelings and thoughts that come up. Don't judge or analyze, just observe. Use the space below to write down your thoughts and insights.

RECLAIMING SPIRIT 1

If I believe that the circumstances are not right or that I don't deserve to be happy, the Universe will agree. As a matter of fact, the Universe always agrees. Therefore, before we unleash our creative powers, it's necessary that we are willing to receive and feel deserving: congruently and now.

Go to your mirror and look yourself in the eyes and say, "I deserve to be happy and healthy," or "I deserve to be in a loving relationship," or anything else you would like to manifest. Do this every day until you really mean it with every cell of your body. In the beginning, the critic inside of you may protest. That is to be expected. Just smile and breathe. Give it time.

RECLAIMING SPIRIT 2

The greatest magicians have conditioned their thoughts so well that they cast, with every exhalation, a very powerful spell into the world: they send thoughts of gratitude. They know that every moment is a seed that encapsulates infinite potentiality. They know that in the moment they can access that potential and mindfully create the next moment. Be convinced that the moment is perfect as is: All is Well.

Go to Chapter 6 and fill out the sections of the *Gratitude List* and the *Transformation and Vision List* for this week.

We are Spirit and so are You.

As with "pop-ups" on the internet,
I find myself fending off the pettiness
Of the "world's" distractions
Fighting a moment to moment battle
To know the "now"
Else like light itself
I am sucked into the black-hole
Of egos "umbilicized" to yesterday
Promising an eternity of stillborn tomorrows
The "enemy" has never been "out there"
It has been my failure to embrace
The "now"

-William

There is more on campus at www.InnerGuidanceNetwork.org:

- ❏ Learn what people need to do who live "out of control lives"
- ❏ Relax deeply and gain new insights with guided meditations

I am Spirit and so are You.

Shine your light today.

You are light

Let your Energy flow freely

Remove any thought that slows your vibration

No Worry

No Doubt

No Fear

There is Only Love

Stay in the Now

Be Fully Present

With open ears

With quiet mind

Your soul will find Peace

Your Truth will emerge

Your light will spiral to new heights

Circling those around you

With Calm

With Peace

With Truth

Patricia Omoqui

I am Spirit
You are Spirit
All is Spirit
and
All is Well

Align with your Original Intent

We live to fully express who we came here to be.

—

You and I and everyone else are in essence Spirit or *Divine Consciousness*. All of us are on a blissful journey of redefining and recreating our own essence. We're all engaged in a continuous process of renewal, and have created earth and the human experience for this purpose.

In *The ClearView Conspiracy* Stephanie says: "It all starts with the intention with which you came into this lifetime. We call it our 'Original Intent.' We all want to fully express who we came here to be. That passion, that desire, that wanting is the first ingredient. It is your magical magnet. It will attract whatever you deeply desire on your journey; all you need to do is align yourself with your original intent and—go with the flow."

Don't worry if you don't have a crisp idea what your Original Intent is. In essence you don't even need to know. But, *do* know that your body is a highly refined guidance system that nudges you in the right direction—all the time. Go in the direction that feels good and gives you a sense of fulfillment.

—

Just before your birth—very much like a painter—you had a vision. You decided to take on physical form and be born into the human experience to joyously create a masterpiece. The circumstances you currently live in are your paints. Don't blame or resist! Use them to manifest what you came here to express. Remember, the masterpiece you intended to create is not physical in nature; *it is pure consciousness*.

Moment of Contemplation

Please get comfortable, close your eyes and let the text sink in. Observe the feelings and thoughts that come up. Don't judge or analyze, just observe. Use the space below to write down your thoughts and insights.

～⎯⎯⎯⎯⎯～

RECLAIMING SPIRIT 1

The following exercise may help you figure out what your Original Intent is. Close your eyes and picture your life. Go to "My Great Moments List" on page 116 and write down five to ten moments or phases in your life when you felt ecstatic, passionate or profoundly happy.

RECLAIMING SPIRIT 2

Review "My Great Moments List." Did you figure out why these moments were so enjoyable? Do you see patterns? Most likely, the underlying vibrational energy has something to do with your Original Intent. How can you integrate this information into your life—now?

RECLAIMING SPIRIT 3

If you had a magic wand, what kind of future would you create? Relax and take your time. Imagine that virtually everything is possible. Where would you like to live? What kind of work would you like to do and what would you like your relationships to be like, your house, hobbies, spirituality, etc? Dream away! Look at the images that come up. Go to Chapter 6 and use a **Dream Sheet** to jot them down.

RECLAIMING SPIRIT 4

Go to Chapter 6 and fill out the sections of the **Gratitude List** and the **Transformation and Vision List** for this week.

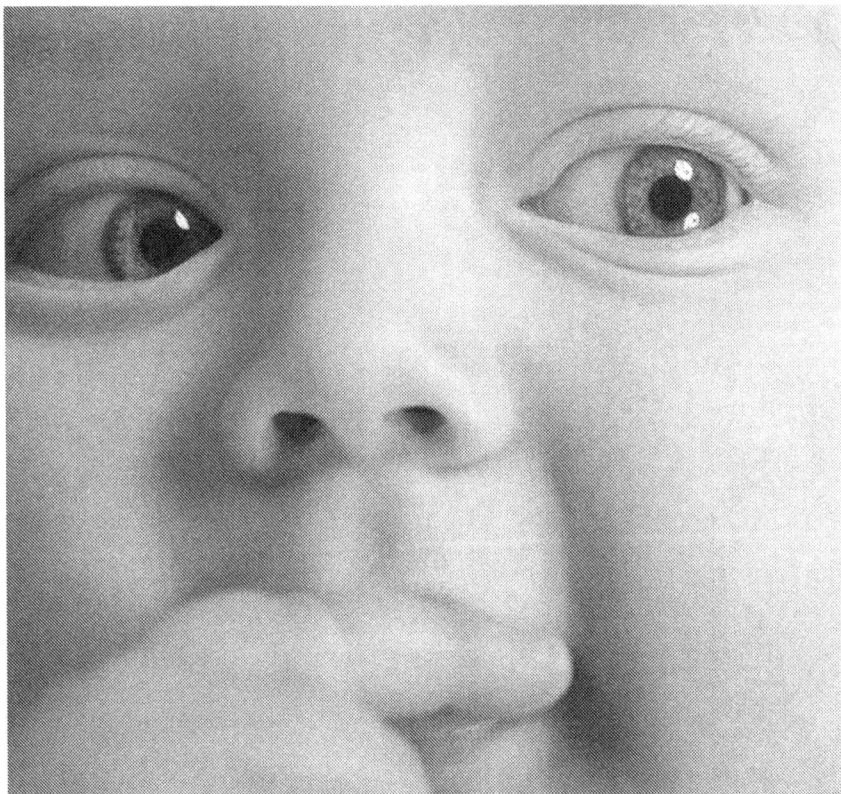

I am Spirit and so are You.

"Over and over again, I see life unfolding as a series of learning experiences, allegories and parables that have been set before me. I believe my purpose is to learn...that we all are here to learn. 'What is my original intent'...to learn and revise, to instruct and reflect, to remember that I am both student and teacher."

- Bill

There is more on campus at www.InnerGuidanceNetwork.org:

❏ Learn about the cosmic Law of Least Resistance

❏ Relax deeply and gain new insights with guided meditations

I am Spirit and so are You.

Express yourself today!

May my life be
A dance of joy
Full of passion
An expression of the beauty
I hold within

May every move I make
Bring delight to those around me
Inspiring them to
Dance their own exuberant dance

Patricia Omoqui

I am Spirit
You are Spirit
All is Spirit
and
All is Well

Step 5

Align with your Inner Guide

We all have an inner guide nudging us along, all the time.

—

Just moments before your birth, you were fully conscious, and you had a clear vision of what you wanted to manifest on earth. By now, you may have forgotten your "Original Intent." That is all right, because you were born with a flawless sense of direction. All you need to do is listen to your Inner Guide.

"But how does my Inner Guide communicate with me?" you may wonder. Well, much like the "hard wired" biological responses that help you survive. When your body needs fluids, you have a *desire* to drink. When you quench your thirst, your body responds with joy and gratitude.

Like water on a hot day, you desire *meaning* in your life and the more you are on track the more joy you experience. You need to do whatever gives you joy and a sense of fulfillment.

Whenever you get inspired: you're on track! Whenever you become passionate or deeply enthusiastic about something: you're on track! Anything that gives you enjoyment is another meaningful step on your journey.

—

You were born with a flawless sense of direction. All you need to do is listen to your Inner Guide and go with the flow. Profound Happiness is found where Joy and Purpose meet.

Moment of Contemplation

Please get comfortable, close your eyes and let the text sink in. Observe the feelings and thoughts that come up. Don't judge or analyze, just observe. Use the space below to write down your thoughts and insights.

∽∼✿∼∽

RECLAIMING SPIRIT 1

This week, be selective! Only (or mostly) give your time and attention to people and situations that give you joy. See what happens.

RECLAIMING SPIRIT 2

Review the Dream Sheet you have worked on last week and go to the *Quality of Life Worksheet* in Chapter 6. Complete only the first column. For each area, write in a couple of words about your dreams and desires. If you could create the life of your dreams, what would that be?

Most happy people have developed balanced lives and are active in all or many of the areas. The Quality of Life Worksheet invites you to look at your life holistically. However, the domains are just suggestions and certain areas may not apply to you. Whatever you write, make it fun! For instance, for a health goal, you may want to rethink "lose twenty pounds." Why? Well, that's no fun. Losing weight could be an action step. It is crucial that you're excited about it. Going on a bicycling vacation in Ireland, that's fun! Or joining a badminton club, or dancing the tango…

RECLAIMING SPIRIT 3

Go to Chapter 6 and fill out the section of the *Gratitude List* and the *Transformation and Vision List* for this week.

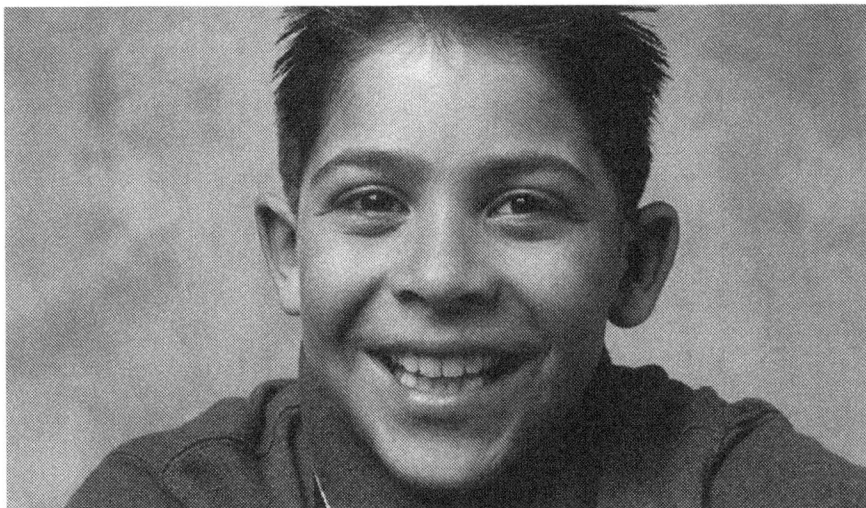

I am Spirit and so are You.

"Connecting with my inner guide... I am constantly reminded of what path is the best or which choice I should make. And when I fail to listen to this inner urge to do things a certain way, I am faced with all types of issues and delays (or) I foul it up, just to see more clearly how I could have avoided the trouble.

"This brings up so much for me. Time and time again, I am guided, I resist or allow other external forces to influence me in another direction. Only to regret it later. Especially when my mind is made up to follow my spirit and I don't anyway. What a sting!

"I guess my stubbornness causes the universe to send me messages to help me on my way to myself. Part of me can tell that I already know what to do. It is all knowing. I am Spirit, All is Spirit and All is love."

- Mikeia

There is more on campus at www.InnerGuidanceNetwork.org:

❏ Learn that how we are guided through life is as simple as a children's game

❏ Relax deeply and gain new insights with guided meditations

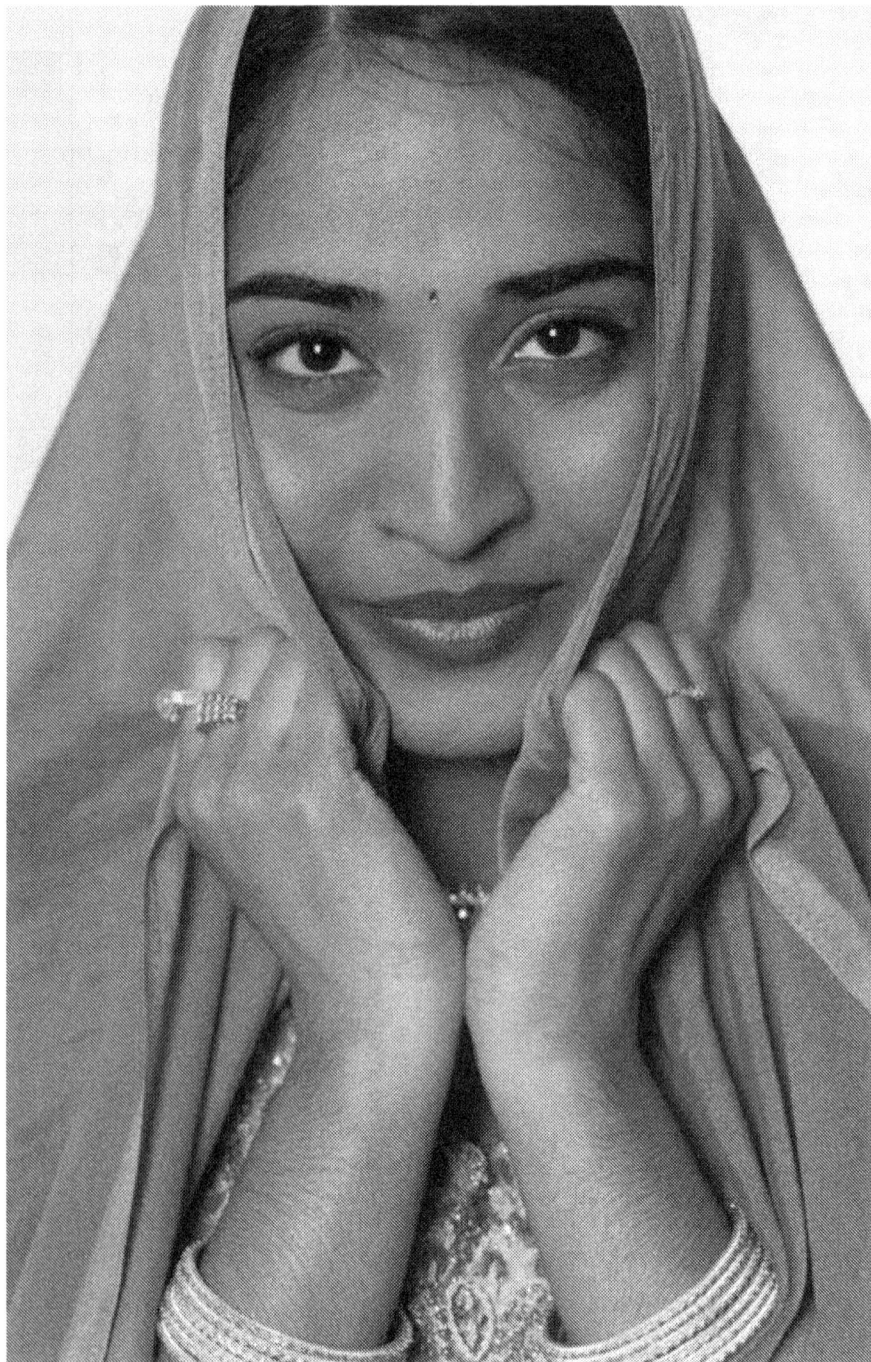

I am Spirit and so are You.

Flow with the current moment.

Breathe

Know
Feel
Believe
Hear Spirit

Hear Spirit
For Spirit speaks to you all the time
You must only relax and listen

Fighting against the current moment
Or living in the past
Or anticipating the future
Causes you to be distracted and
Then you can't hear Spirit's voice.

The more you relax into
The eternal moment,
The eternal, infinite now
The louder Spirit's voice becomes

The more pain you release,
The louder and clearer Spirit's voice becomes
The more you laugh and rejoice,
The more clearly you will hear Spirit's voice

Patricia Omoqui

I am Spirit
You are Spirit
All is Spirit
and
All is Well

Create a Goal Plan

By putting your wishes to paper you will increase the likelihood of reaching your dreams a thousand fold.

—

Studies have shown that when we write down our goals and dreams, we are far more likely to reach them.

In order to mindfully create a fulfilling and joyful existence—*and not leave the circumstances of your life to chance*—it is very important to first figure out what you want to create. While being grateful for the now, look ahead and wonder how you would like your next moment to be. Focus your mind and visualize. How would you like to feel when you exhale your next breath… a*nd the next…and the next…and the next?*

By doing this, you set the stage for the real magic to unfold. While you are thinking about your dreams and writing them down, you focus your mind on that which you desire. The more consistently you do this and let your vision dance on the rhythm of your passion, the more you send forth a powerful energy into the Universe. Know for a fact that the Universe is eager to respond to your message and wants to "fill the order."

—

From a place of groundedness in the moment, cast your eyes into the future. What would you like to manifest three or six months from now? Write it down and be as specific as possible. By doing this, you are putting in an order, and the Universe will deliver. But remember, if you give a vague or unclear order, you may end up with the wrong food on your plate!

Moment of Contemplation

Please get comfortable, close your eyes and let the text sink in. Observe the feelings and thoughts that come up. Don't judge or analyze, just observe. Use the space below to write down your thoughts and insights.

RECLAIMING SPIRIT 1

This week, you are encouraged to roll up your sleeves and put your desires to paper. Please review the *Quality of Life Worksheet* that you partly filled out last week. Remember, the worksheet is just a tool to invite you to look at your life holistically. Certain areas may not apply, while other categories may be more important to you. Feel free to adjust.

RECLAIMING SPIRIT 2

In the second column, write down per area what specific goals you want to reach within 3 months. For instance, you want to ride your bike 3 times a week, get in shape, get a new bicycle after you have lost 10 pounds and ... plan your vacation. "Rockies, here I come!" Be creative and make sure it's fun.

RECLAIMING SPIRIT 3

Review the worksheet. In the third column, prioritize your goals— with your heart. Pick your top five.

RECLAIMING SPIRIT 4

Go to Chapter 6 and fill out the section of the *Gratitude List* and the *Transformation and Vision List* for this week.

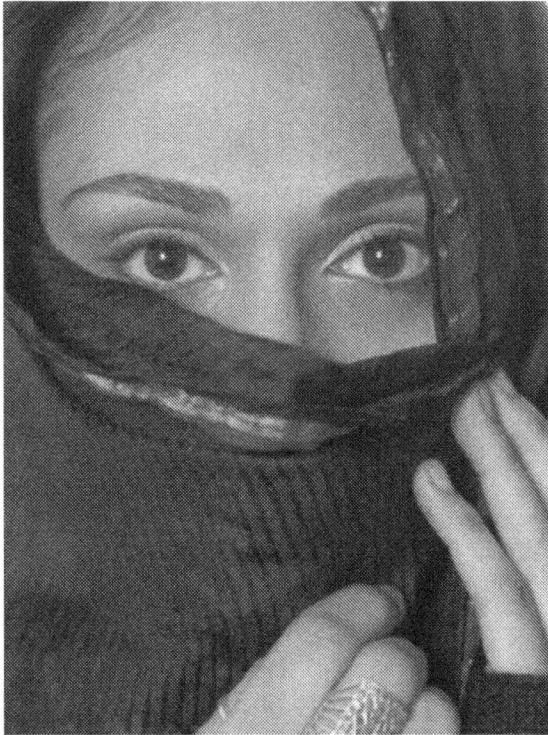

I am Spirit and so are You.

"I always felt there is something here that I needed to know. When my first husband and I built this huge home in upstate NY, one night after we moved in, I just sat on the steps and cried. I just knew this was not right, I should've been happy, but something deep inside told me, this would be a sad place. I just knew it would be the beginning of something very bad for us. Money or lack thereof, took its toll on our marriage, made my husband severely ill, and was the main cause for our divorce. We lost everything. I am sure the signs were there, but I didn't know. Or didn't see until it was too late. My ego had been too strong. Now, I have learned to listen to the spirit inside of me, and pay attention. Thank you for this wonderful book."

- C.S.

There is more on campus at www.InnerGuidanceNetwork.org:

❏ Learn more about the Law of Attraction

❏ Learn the 4 essential qualities of a successful goal plan

❏ Relax deeply and gain new insights with guided meditations

I am Spirit and so are You.

If you could know with certainty that every experience on your life path is perfect, how would your reactions to your circumstances change?

Perfection of your life's path

Is to know that you are truly you – in all ways

In joy is this

In truth is this

For you are this:

Perfect, pure love

Energy

Emanating

Beating

Pulsing from your heart

Deeper than your heart

A space in the Center, the very center of your being

Unlock this

Discover

Configure

Reconfigure your life

To match who you Truly are

In

Your

Essential

Essence

Patricia Omoqui

I am Spirit
You are Spirit
All is Spirit
and
All is Well

Take Charge: The R-Factor

If we want to create the life we desire, we must take full responsibility for our thoughts, feelings and actions. It is the only way to transform the drama in our lives into Divine opportunities for spiritual growth.

—

In *The ClearView Conspiracy*, Chiquita talks about the kind of responsibility that makes or breaks the quality of our lives, regulates the drama-soup around us and creates peace in the world. She says, "[...] virtually everything that 'gives' us a strong emotional response, such as anger, sadness or fear, has nothing to do with the outside world. These emotions indicate that parts of us are bruised, insecure and still unconscious. We are triggered and must assume complete responsibility. Blaming others for our emotional imbalance will only perpetuate the drama. Whenever we are triggered, we must stop and take responsibility."

It's similar to having someone accidentally bump against your bruised arm. It's not the person who bumps into you, who caused the pain; no... it's your bruise. And the pain is really a blessing, because it reminds you to take care of your bruise.

When life is getting hard and painful, it usually indicates that we are paddling upstream. Let's not blame the river for flowing toward the ocean, it is meant to go there—*and so are you*. Only you can turn the boat around. It's your *responsibility*.

—

If you want to assume your role as powerful creator, you must take full responsibility for all your thoughts, feelings and actions. You must remember that you and your circumstances are products of your own creation. You are in charge!

Moment of Contemplation

Please get comfortable, close your eyes and let the text sink in. Observe the feelings and thoughts that come up. Don't judge or analyze, just observe. Use the space below to write down your thoughts and insights.

∽∞∽

RECLAIMING SPIRIT 1

Dear friend, this week, I would like to invite you to look at your bruises: your sensitive spots. Why? Well, because it probably points to areas in which you have been paddling upstream. You may find deeply rooted fears and realize that you have been resisting and holding on. Go to Chapter 6 and fill out the *My Bruises* sheet.

RECLAIMING SPIRIT 2

Review your *Quality of Life* worksheet and select your two most important goals. Go to Chapter 6 and fill out two *Goal Plans*.

RECLAIMING SPIRIT 3

Go to Chapter 6 and fill out the section of the *Gratitude List* and the *Transformation and Vision List* for this week.

I am Spirit and so are You.

"Thanks for the suggestion to work with one of my predominant triggers. Holding the emotional response in an accepting and nonjudgmental way while breathing into it worked beautifully. My highly charged, emotional response quickly transformed into a very manageable form with mild emotional elements and helpful insights. I'm looking forward to applying this technique when this issue gets triggered in a real life situation."

- Dr. James Strohl

<u>There is more on campus at www.InnerGuidanceNetwork.org:</u>

❑ Learn how you can stop your daily struggles—*immediately*

❑ Relax deeply and gain new insights with guided meditations

I am Spirit and so are You.

As you become consciously aware that you create your life, you begin to make better and better choices with your thoughts. Your life is your creation. Own your life. Own your thoughts.

Each moment

Consciously or Not

You are creating your life

What you are living is not a mistake

It is your creation

Stop

Know

You can become a Conscious Creator

With an awareness of your thoughts

Begin to choose those thoughts of

>   Love

>   Joy

>   Peace

>   Abundance

>   Hope

Hold those thoughts

Do not turn back

To your old patterns of thinking

For your thoughts hold power

The Power to create your life

Patricia Omoqui

I am Spirit
You are Spirit
All is Spirit
and
All is Well

Step 8

Create Mindfully:
The Art of Mindful Creation

**Every thought is the beginning of a new creation,
and our passion gives it life.**

—

The most powerful cosmic law that impacts our lives is *The Law of Attraction.* As soon as we understand this law and align ourselves with this mind boggling force we become powerful creators, able of creating the life we deeply desire.

Everyone creates, but only a few create mindfully. Whether you like it or not, you are a powerful spiritual wizard, yet many of us are unaware of it. We are like apprentice magicians who create monsters instead of butterflies. We create disarray instead of harmony, wars instead of peace, illness instead of health. We're misusing our magical powers and we're complaining about the reality we have created.

What is the magical formula? Well, it all starts with a thought. Every thought is the beginning of a new creation, but that is not enough. We need to feed it energy. How do we do that?

In *The ClearView Conspiracy*, Lakshmi says, "You can feed your thoughts focus, time, joy and expectation. The more you passionately think and talk about what you want, visualize it and expect it to materialize, the more birthing power you'll give it."

—

With every thought, you send a vibrational message into the Universe. The more congruent your thought is, and the more you give it passion and time, the more likely it is that you will attract what you desire.

Moment of Contemplation

Please get comfortable, close your eyes and let the text sink in. Observe the feelings and thoughts that come up. Don't judge or analyze, just observe. Use the space below to write down your thoughts and insights.

The Seven Steps of
the Art of Mindful Creation

►**1.** Every morning and every night—*and as often as possible throughout your day*—go within and ask yourself how you can increase meaning and joy into your existence. Imagine what that could be until you get a smile on your face and can formulate **a *clear intention*** of what you want to create.

►**2.** *Focus* on your creation process. Make it one of the most important things you do. Surround yourself with images of what you want to create. Make a collage or vision board. Remind yourself throughout the day of what you want to manifest (a sticky note on your computer, a card in your purse, or an email to yourself), talk about it, dream about it, imagine that you already have acquired it—and be delighted!

►**3.** Give as much *time* as possible to your creation process. Give it quality time!

►**4.** Have *fun* with it. Your thought and intention give the creation process direction, but your *emotion* gives it life.

►**5.** *Expect,* beyond a shadow of a doubt, that whatever you want to create will come into being.

►**6.** Avoid getting too wrapped up in the steps. *Release* the details to the Universe. Sit back and trust. Do this before going to sleep.

►**7.** *Keep the process going.* Every morning start again with Step 1.

RECLAIMING SPIRIT 1

Dear friend, this week, I would like to invite you to combine your *Goal Plans* with *The Seven Steps of the Art of Mindful Creation*. Twice a day, reflect on your goal plan and implement the Seven Steps. Make it a routine. Do this for four weeks and I would love to hear from you. I am certain that you will be amazed by what you have created.

RECLAIMING SPIRIT 2

Review your *Goal Plans* and check to see if you are on track. If necessary, make adjustments.

RECLAIMING SPIRIT 3

Get out a stack of magazines, glue and a pair of scissors. Go to Chapter 6 and find the *Collage Page*. With your *Goal Plans* in mind, have fun creating a visual of what you want to manifest.

.RECLAIMING SPIRIT 4

Go to Chapter 6 and fill out the section of the *Gratitude List* and the *Transformation and Vision List* for this week.

"I don't understand why we are all so afraid to do what feels right. Why do we fear it so much, when, when we listen to that voice, we are more peaceful, calm and happy? I think that it may be most people don't think they deserve happiness. Well, that is exactly why I want to open a Spiritualist Center. To make people see their greatness. To see their talents, to remind them what they already know. We all know, we are born this way. Just somewhere along the way, we lost sight. It's time we all see again."

- Lori

There is more on campus at www.InnerGuidanceNetwork.org:

❑ Get answers to questions such as: "I do what you tell me to do, but it still doesn't work. Why?"

❑ Relax deeply and gain new insights with guided meditations

I am Spirit and so are You.

Open up and just be willing to follow your heart. Miracles flow from this space.

Be willing
That is all

Spirit will help you with all the details
You will be joyful when you
See the results of what Spirit has in store for you
For those who surround you

You will be a blessing to all you connect with
You are willingly ready
To be a conduit of truth
Of love
Of abundance
Of hope
Of all good things to all people

Patricia Omoqui

I am Spirit
You are Spirit
All is Spirit
and
All is Well

I AM A POWERFUL CREATOR

Send in your success stories! We are especially interested in stories that reflect the use of the Art of Mindful Creation. Your story may be selected and posted on the website and published in Spirits Onymous Handbook 2009. Please, submit your story electronically on the website. Teena Snoo submitted this wonderful little story:

TAFFIES AND A YACHT

Spirits Onymous and The Secret were new to me. I began to notice what I called "coincidences" happening at least once a day. I would like to tell you about what happened on a weekend in May. I guess, the universe wanted to showed me that I am a powerful creator and able to shape my reality.

While I was driving home from my favorite store, I thought about many things. I thought about giving my students taffies and better prizes to use as rewards. I am an elementary school teacher you see. I thought of things I needed to do and of things I hadn't done before. I thought about taking the West train to the city, since I've never rode on it. I thought about going to a park that I passed and about yachts. *Yes,* I thought, *I want to go on a yacht!*

The next day (Sunday), a friend called in the morning and said, "Let's go to the boat show. We can take the train near my house."

He was referring to the train I wanted to ride. I was flabbergasted and we agreed to meet at the station. On my way to the door, I remembered that a "bed buddy heat pack" had ripped open and that rice had spilled onto the bedroom floor. I decided to quickly vacuum the floor. Vacuuming took longer than I anticipated and I got to the train station a few minutes late. We missed the train. But no problem, instead of waiting at the station, we decided to check out the park! The park was nice; it even had ducks.

At the boat show, my friend wanted information about boat insurances. When I took a handful of taffies from this display, the rep was a little surprised. I explained that I was a teacher and would give the taffies to my students. Without saying a word, he took out a big bag with at least three hundred taffies. As the day progressed, vendors gave me hats, key chains, T-shirts, beach balls and erasable note pads: items that could be used as rewards for my students. And to top it off, I even got on a yacht. Unfortunately, it didn't go anywhere. But then again, I never specifically said I wanted the yacht to be sailing in water. I must learn to be more specific in my requests.

Teena

Reach Enlightenment Now

Recognize eternal perfection in each moment.

—

In *The ClearView Conspiracy*, Moses says, "We must realize that we can reach enlightenment within one single breath ... and that we can lose it within one single breath, as well. Enlightenment is not the status quo. It can't be checked off of our to-do list. Enlightenment refers to a level of consciousness that can be reached every moment of the day, moment-by-moment, right now ... and now ... and now ... and now.

"During every exhalation, you have the choice to live your next breath in a state of spiritual consciousness ... or not. During every moment, you have the choice to embrace your true Self and see Spirit in all living things ... or not. The choice is yours. Between every thought, there is a pause ... a smidgen of space. Step into that void and direct your next thought. What is it going to be? Will your next moment be spent consciously? Enlightenment is merely a breath away. It's a process of choice and created one moment at a time: now...and now...now... now...now."

Mankind is engaged in a never-ending process of renewal. Our purpose is not to accomplish anything of material value, but to partake in an eternal process of Divine rejuvenation. We will never get it done!

—

The object of our existence is not a distant state of eternal bliss; it is the recognition of eternal bliss in each and every moment.

Moment of Contemplation

Please get comfortable, close your eyes and let the text sink in. Observe the feelings and thoughts that come up. Don't judge or analyze, just observe. Use the space below to write down your thoughts and insights.

⌒⌒⌒⌒〜⊛〜⌒⌒⌒

RECLAIMING SPIRIT 1

You are encouraged to develop methods that will remind you—*throughout your day*—to stop, and reach enlightenment during your next breath.

RECLAIMING SPIRIT 2

In our home, we have a "mindfulness bowl," which rings every 15 minutes. The ringing of the bowl reminds us to stop and refocus on the here and now. When the bowl rings, we take a deep breath, and gently bring our lives back into perspective: I am Spirit, You are Spirit, All is Spirit and All is Well.

Go to www.InnerGuidanceNetwork.org and click on the tiny bowl, immediately under The InnerGuidance Network logo.

RECLAIMING SPIRIT 3

Review your *Goal Plans* and check to see if you are on track. If necessary, make adjustments.

RECLAIMING SPIRIT 4

Go to Chapter 6 and fill out the section of the *Gratitude List* and the *Transformation and Vision List* for this week.

We are Spirit and so are You.

"When we look at the world and ourselves through the innocent eyes of a child, perhaps the true meaning of Freedom does in that moment, reveal itself, almost effortlessly. Indeed, we can KNOW (beyond belief) that we are Spirit, and that ALL IS SPIRIT. To meet with others in this inquiry into ourselves, is a genuinely rare and sacred opportunity."

- Mike

There is more on campus at www.InnerGuidanceNetwork.org:

❑ Learn that not even God can afford to be stagnant

❑ Relax deeply and gain new insights with guided meditations

I am Spirit and so are You.

Begin to see every circumstance of your life as perfect.

An amazing Awakening

Be Happy

Be Patient

Be Excited

Do your Moment-by-Moment work of

Waking up

There is much to look forward to

Much to enjoy

Be in the Now each moment

Become aware of what is really happening

Below the sorrow and the fear

This is only surface

Deep beneath

You will find

Beauty and growth

Beyond anything you can presently imagine

All is truly perfect

Decide to accept that as Fact

You will begin to see the whole world

And everyone in it

In a brand new and

Exquisitely beautiful light

Patricia Omoqui

I am Spirit
You are Spirit
All is Spirit
and
All is Well

Be a Mindful Leader

**Be mindful of the fact that your vibrational energy impacts the lives of
thousands of people around you—directly and indirectly.
We are all leaders, continuously shaping the future of mankind.**

—

A collective consciousness is breaking through that will pull humanity into
an age of spiritual awareness, peace and purpose. We are reaching critical
mass!

You are invited to fulfill a Mindful Leadership role in this process, in
whatever societal function you may have: parent, teacher, mechanic.
Mindful Leaders see the brilliance and perfection in all human beings and
in all situations. All is Spirit and All is Well.

In *The ClearView Conspiracy* John says, "I've learned that with every
thought, I set into motion a chain reaction of events that will support or
obstruct the quality of my life and the lives of thousands of people around
me. We owe it to ourselves, and the rest of humanity to celebrate our
greatness and see greatness in all we meet."

When we are drawn into gossip and drama, become aware of that, stop,
and step back. And when people around us indulge in drama, we will not
join them. Instead, we will gently ask them to refocus on what they want to
create.

—

**Mindful Leaders lead by example. The more we express ourselves
fully and follow our dreams, the more we motivate others to do the
same. Let's not play small any longer, let's shine and let's support
others to shine as well. After all, that's what we came here to do.**

Moment of Contemplation

Please get comfortable, close your eyes and let the text sink in. Observe the feelings and thoughts that come up. Don't judge or analyze, just observe. Use the space below to write down your thoughts and insights.

RECLAIMING SPIRIT 1

Hone your #1 Mindful Leadership skill: SMILE, and cast a light of gratitude on as many people as possible. Let them know that you see their greatness and that you appreciate them as they are, not as you would like them to be. There is only one condition: You must speak from your heart and mean it! See their greatness. See their beauty.

RECLAIMING SPIRIT 2

Review your *Goal Plans* and check to see if you are on track. If necessary, make adjustments.

RECLAIMING SPIRIT 3

Take a moment and look back on your achievements so far. Please go to Chapter 6 and write on your accomplishments page the insights you have gained, the relationships that you have created and the small and big successes you have reached. In what areas has your life become more focused, enjoyable and fulfilling?

RECLAIMING SPIRIT 4

Go to Chapter 6 and fill out the section of the *Gratitude List* and the *Transformation and Vision List* for this week.

I am Spirit and so are You.

"The Mindful Leader helps the people around him or her discover their innate intelligence, bravery, and joy."

- Joan

There is more on campus at www.InnerGuidanceNetwork.org:

- ❏ Learn the four core principles of Mindful Leadership
- ❏ Relax deeply and gain new insights with guided meditations

I am Spirit and so are You.

Allow the Divine Light to shine from within you.

I move myself out of the way

And merge with the Source of All that is

Trusting

That messages will flow through me

To those who need to hear and

Are ready to embrace New Truth

Divine Light

Shine inside me

So others can bask in the Radiance

The warmth of Love

Gentleness of spirit,

Strength of Full, Unencumbered Power

Flow, let my Spirit flow

Let my life flow

Let my heart merge with those around me so

We embrace the commonality between us,

The human Divinity of our beings

Delight

In each glimpse you see of this

Miraculous New Way of Being

Smile in Peace

Knowing that you can never turn from this Truth

This Truth will release you from all suffering

Patricia Omoqui, Copyright Patricia G. Omoqui 2007, All Rights Reserved

I am Spirit
You are Spirit
All is Spirit
and
All is Well

Step 11

Manifest Physical Resilience

Celebrate and access the amazing healing potential of the body.

–

If you want to improve the quality of your life, further define your spiritual path and reach for profound happiness, it is imperative to respect your body. All is Spirit, your body included.

We are graced with an awesome instrument with which we navigate through this physical realm. Stop for a moment and realize how utterly amazing your body is: how it regulates temperature, digests foods, infuses oxygen into your bloodstream, relays messages throughout your body and communicates with you about what feels right or wrong. Your body is your temple and the seat of your Inner Guide. You are perfect as you are. You are whole and healthy. It is your natural state.

Your Inner Guide communicates with you in many languages; however, the primary means of communication is your body. It is important to pay attention to how your body feels, physically and emotionally. Listen to your body and honor what it is telling you.

–

Your body provides you with a flawless guidance system, guiding you to create the life you were born to live and maintain physical resilience. Be quiet, go within and listen to what your body is telling you. What does your body need? It's whispering something to you, right now.

Moment of Contemplation

Please get comfortable, close your eyes and let the text sink in. Observe the feelings and thoughts that come up. Don't judge or analyze, just observe. Use the space below to write down your thoughts and insights.

RECLAIMING SPIRIT 1

I would like to invite you to become mindful about what your body is telling you. Slow down—and listen. Are you taking a deep breath every 15 minutes? When you do, go inside and ask your body what it needs. Do this for a week. You will be astounded.

RECLAIMING SPIRIT 2

Review your *Goal Plans* and check to see if you are on track. If necessary, make adjustments.

RECLAIMING SPIRIT 3

Go to Chapter 6 and review what you wrote on your accomplishments page and add any other successes, big and small, that come to mind. In what areas has your life become more focused, enjoyable and fulfilling?

RECLAIMING SPIRIT 4

Go to Chapter 6 and fill out the section of the *Gratitude List* and the *Transformation and Vision List* for this week.

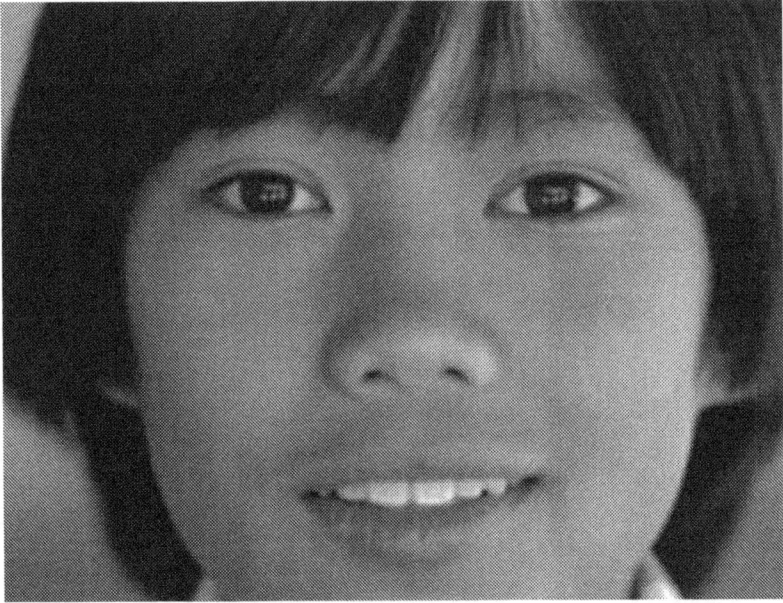

I am Spirit and so are You.

"I have recently been working with a different image as I eat - imagining the food that enters my mouth as food; i.e., apples, toast, broccoli etc, and watching the gradual merger as the 'food' is integrated into my cells. What I find happens as a result is that I select food more carefully!!"

-Kit

"After doing this exercise, I realized that I have not been very still, and have become ungrounded. I HAVE to take the time to become quiet and listen to my body and soul. It's so good to stay in check."

- L

There is more on campus at www.InnerGuidanceNetwork.org:

❑ Learn the first thing you need to do to create physical resilience

❑ Relax deeply and gain new insights with guided meditations

I am Spirit and so are You.

Envision yourself today standing in a stream of bright, cleansing, Universal Light. Feel the light wash over your being. Feel the changes that come, allowing this light to surround and fill you.

Bathe your soul in

Streams of Light

Uncover anything that

You need to release

You have released so much already

Just trust

The rest will fall away

You will emerge new

A Chrysalis

You will find your true beauty

Your spirit will be freed

You will soar to new heights

Laugh

Let your heart be full of joy

Fly

Like the Monarch Butterfly

Patricia Omoqui

I am Spirit
You are Spirit
All is Spirit
and
All is Well

Step 12

Support a Sustainable World

Let the world be an expression of our internal balance.

—

The world we live in is an indication of our own vibrational energy. The world mirrors our internal state of harmony. So, what is it mirroring? What does the world say about humanity? What does the world say about you?

If it is up to you—*and it is up to you*—what would you like to change in the world? ...

Now, apply that wish to your own life and become the change you (wish to) see in the world. Focus on yourself; the world will follow. Lasting change only happens one soul at a time, beginning with you.

Curb the tendency to start a war against global warming. Instead, recognize the warning signs, and stay focused on *what you want to create*: a sustainable world, in which we live in harmony with nature. Let the world become an expression of your own internal balance.

—

What can you do to increase your internal balance and create a more respectful relationship with the world you live in? What can you do today, tomorrow?

Moment of Contemplation

Please get comfortable, close your eyes and let the text sink in. Observe the feelings and thoughts that come up. Don't judge or analyze, just observe. Use the space below to write down your thoughts and insights.

RECLAIMING SPIRIT 1

Rent the movie "An Inconvenient Truth" and go to the website www.climatecrisis.net. There are many easy things you can do that will improve your relationship with nature. Be the change you (wish to) see in the world.

RECLAIMING SPIRIT 2

Review your *Goal Plans* and check to see if you are on track. If necessary, make adjustments.

RECLAIMING SPIRIT 3

Go to Chapter 6 and fill out the section of the *Gratitude List* and the *Transformation and Vision List* for this week.

RECLAIMING SPIRIT 4

Go to Chapter 6 and review what you wrote on your accomplishments page and write your success story! Send it in. We may place it on the web or in next year's handbook. We look forward to hearing from you.

I am Spirit and so are You

"Sometimes it can be scary, because being aware means you then have to take action. It can be hard to change. As in any transition, you learn so much about yourself and are out of your comfort zone, establishing a new one. Which is always easier said than done. But the gain is tremendous. So the more you make the time to be with yourself, the happier, calmer, more peaceful of a person you become. With that, we can change the world."

- Lori

There is more on campus at www.InnerGuidanceNetwork.org:

❑ Learn why you don't want to be a frog in warm water

❑ Relax deeply and gain new insights with guided meditations

I am Spirit and so are You

Are you ready to be the change you envision in the world?

I am infused with vibrancy
Bright, pure light shines through
The windows of my Soul, my eyes
I share my energy freely
Through hugs, smiles, caring touches
To those I meet on life's path

I am a light in my world
Inspired living flows through me
Passionate dreams
Magnificently Rising above seeming hurdles
I live my life
Freely
Easily
Deliberately
Lovingly
Happily
Joyously
Refreshingly

I am the change I envision in the world

Patricia Omoqui

I am Spirit
You are Spirit
All is Spirit
and
All is Well

Chapter 4

SPIRITS ONYMOUS MEETINGS

The mission and structure

Mission

The Spirits Onymous meetings offer a time and place for members of The InnerGuidance Network to meet. Anyone who believes that we are Spirit having a human experience, and those who would like to explore that notion, are welcomed. During the meetings, the participants contemplate and discuss the twelve Spirits Onymous principles, meditate, and make commitments for the following week. The participants support each other in expressing their true nature and in joyfully creating the life they desire to live. Additionally, peer-coaching relationships among the members are created.

Vision

Spirits Onymous meetings are offered in rapidly increasing numbers throughout the world, providing the same inviting and supportive structure.

Location of the meetings

Open meetings, which are published on the InnerGuidance website and in local publications, must be organized in public locations, such as schools, libraries, churches, health centers, stores, and hotels. Closed meetings may be offered in private homes. Participation in closed meetings is by invitation only and the groups are typically no larger than six individuals.

Frequency of the meetings

It is recommended to meet bi-weekly and throughout the year. This way, the frequency is not too taxing and it offers a high level of flexibility. The meetings should run parallel with the on-line course, where a new principle is released every week. So, if it is a "meeting week", the group discusses the same principle as the on-line course and possibly a brief review of the previous week's material.

During the "off weeks," the participants read the course material and contact their peer-coach to discuss their progress and give and receive support. Peer-coaching is typically done by phone.

Ideally, the bi-weekly meetings are hosted on the weeks that the even principles (2, 4, 6, 8, 10, 12) are released on-line; however, this is not required. The host/facilitator has the option to adjust to local preferences.

Host

The host is the person who takes the initiative and organizes the meeting. He or she is responsible for the financial and organizational aspects of running the group. The host determines time and location, and is the contact person for The InnerGuidance Network (IGN). Anyone who would like to host a meeting contacts the IGN and signs a simple agreement, addressing basic ethical and philosophical principles. Go to www.InnerGuidanceNetwork.org and click on "Spirits Onymous" and on "Host a local Meeting" for the latest registration information.

Facilitator

The facilitator is a function, not so much a specific person. It is strongly encouraged that the facilitator role is shared by at least three people who take turns. The host is usually one of the facilitators. Facilitators must be Certified Peer-Coaches. For requirements, see below. Facilitators make sure that the structure of the meeting is maintained and encourage participants to find answers within. Instead of teaching, facilitators support, paraphrase and ask open questions.

Peer-Coaching

You are encouraged to register for the Art of Mindful Communication workshop if it is offered in your area. If that is not possible, go to the website and register for the online course. Completion of the Art of Mindful Communication workshop and the Spirits Onymous course (12 weeks) entitles you to a certificate of Peer-Coaching. Check the website for specifics.

Basic format for a Peer-Coaching session:

❑ Typically, the peer-coach starts with, "What would you like to create this week?" During peer-coaching time at the meeting, the peer-coach may start with an open question, such as, "If you had a magic wand, what kind of future would you create?"

❑ The peer-coach first and foremost *listens*. He offers support and assists the "client" in becoming clearer with open questions or just by repeating a couple of words.

❑ The peer-coach refrains from "taking over." She will give no advice or divert to her own story. The focus is entirely on "the client."

- At the end of the session, the peer-coach asks "the client" what he wants to commit to during the coming week. At the next meeting, the peer-coach will ask "the client" to report on how it went.

- The roles are exchanged and the peer-coach becomes "the client."

Usher

At larger open meetings, it is recommended that an usher is assigned who will facilitate a smooth reception of new people.

Introduction of the meetings

To promote the meetings, the host may decide to organize an introduction presentation two to four weeks before the first meeting. Check the website for available presentation materials.

Spirits Onymous Handbook

The handbook is included in the course fee (six meetings). Guests and those who join half-way are encouraged to purchase one.

Duration of the meetings

The meetings last 1.5 – 2 hours; however, the host may opt to adjust the length of the meeting.

Format of the meetings

Although it is important that the structure of the meetings is recognizable wherever Spirits Onymous meetings are conducted, adjustments can be made to accommodate local preferences. There are three basic meeting formats: a Share Meeting, a Coaching Meeting, and a Grand Meeting. The components are discussed later in this chapter.

Share Meeting
Opening song, five minute meditation and reading from CD
Welcome and discussion
Transformation Sequence
Individual Sharing
Closure

Coaching Meeting
Opening song, five minute meditation and reading from CD
Welcome and discussion
Group splits up into peer-coaching pairs
Individual Sharing (short version)
Closure

Grand Meeting *(typically 2 hours)*
Opening song, meditation and reading from CD
Welcome and discussion
Group splits up into peer-coaching pairs
Transformation Sequence
Individual Sharing
Closure

Timeliness

The host and facilitator must commit to timeliness. Start and finish times must be adhered to as much as possible.

Pagers and cell phones

Pagers and cell phones must be switched off. If participants are on-call (doctors, crisis workers) devices must be switched to vibrate. In case of emergency, calls must be answered outside the meeting space.

Advice giving

To respect each other's individual paths and inner wisdom, participants are asked to refrain from giving unsolicited advice. The premise is to encourage the person to find and trust his or her own innate wisdom.

Blaming and venting

Although it may be helpful at times to vent about a particular situation, Spirits Onymous meetings are not the place to do that. While participants may share their feelings regarding a particular experience, it is imperative that no one is blamed. If a participant wants to explore and share a situation that triggered him, the focus is on recognizing the feeling, owning the feeling and valuing the situation as an opportunity for spiritual growth. The member is encouraged to explore what the situation invites him to manifest.

CD

The Spirits Onymous meeting facilitation CDs can be ordered at the Inner Guidance Network website.

We are Spirit and so are You.

"What a warm and inviting group. I was very pleased to find other 'real world' people who are seeking for connection, peace and meaning. This is a much-needed Soul nourishing respite in my hectic life. I am awed by the connection and diverse "oneness" we create together. I feel renewed, nurtured and affirmed."

- Melissa

"I thought it was very comfortable, relaxing, and everyone there was really supposed to be there. I enjoyed the sharing and the open spirit filled atmosphere."

- Patti

"A warm, caring, family-like atmosphere, a gathering of like-minded people who are gathered together to share the Highest Truth: I am Spirit, you are Spirit, All is Spirit, and All is Well! A remarkable oasis in the desert of ordinary, fast-paced, mundane life!! Hard to find groups of this caliber. Thank you!!"

- Michael

Meeting Structure of a "Grand Meeting"

Facilitator Opens

The facilitator briefly welcomes the participants: "Welcome to Spirits Onymous. My name is Mary, I am Spirit <u>and so are You</u>. Please take a minute and write on your gratitude list what you are grateful for."

The facilitator gives the group a minute for this assignment. She continues with: "Now, go to the Transformation and Vision List and fill out this week's section: one minute."

Again, the facilitator gives the group a minute to complete this task, after which she says, "Please, get comfortable, sit back and re—lax." (See facilitator's prompt card on page 112.) Then she starts the CD, playing the track for that specific week.

Opening Song, Meditation and Reading

The tracks consist of the opening song, "Blessing to the World" by Karen Drucker, followed by a guided meditation and a reading by Adrianus, addressing a Spirits Onymous principle. After the reading, the facilitator stops the CD player.

Welcome and Discussion

The facilitator greets the participants in this fashion (see facilitator's prompt card). "Welcome. We are here to shed our anonymity and embrace our true nature. I am Spirit, You are Spirit, All is Spirit and All is Well. Participants of this meeting will maintain confidentiality and refrain from giving unsolicited advice."

The facilitator makes some short announcements and rereads the last paragraph of the reading. A 15-minute time limitation is given for the discussion. The time limit may be altered at the discretion of the host/facilitator. The facilitator starts the discussion with, "Okay, let's take 15 minutes to discuss. How is this principle relevant to you? What came up during the reading? Who wants to start?"

Peer-Coaching

Following the 15-minutes discussion, the facilitator breaks the group into pairs to offer time for peer-coaching. Initially, it is expected that the facilitator will give specific directions. The pairs may assist each other in filling out and reviewing their Transformation and Vision Sheets, their Quality of Life sheets, or Goal Plans.

As the members are participating longer, they may use this peer-coaching time any way that is helpful. Depending on the size and the available time, the facilitator may assign 10 to 15 minutes. The pairs may agree to continue the peer-coaching process and set up a telephone session or meet in person. This is encouraged.

The Transformation and Vision Sequence

Following the peer-coaching segment, the facilitator calls the participants back into a circle and continues: "Next, we will listen to 'The Transformation and Vision Sequence.' After that, we will have a chance to share." The facilitator starts the Transformation and Vision Sequence on the CD. This guided meditation helps the participants to:

❏ Further relax and focus

❏ Process any unpleasant feelings of the past week and transition into a higher vibrational energy

❏ Envision what they want to manifest the coming week

Sharing and Support

After the Transformation and Vision Sequence, the facilitator passes out the "share card" (page 114) and the "response card" (page 115) and reminds the group how much sharing time each individual has (see sharing time schedule on page 113). The person who receives the "response card" sits opposite to the person with the "share card." When the group is new, it is advisable that the facilitator starts the sharing to "set the tone."

The person who shares may talk about:

❏ Something she is grateful for

❏ Thoughts related to the meditation and/or reading

❏ A possible stressful situation that offered an opportunity for spiritual growth

❏ What she wants to manifest the coming week

When the person is sharing, the facilitator keeps an eye on the time. After the allotted time, the facilitator may hit the chime to let the speaker know that time is up. When the speaker is done, the person with the response card leads the group in affirming the greatness of the speaker. He reads, "Mary, we unconditionally love and support you." The group repeats. He continues with, "You are a wise and powerful creator!" The group repeats. And he concludes with, "You are Spirit and All is Well." The group repeats. The facilitator hits the chime and the group members close their eyes and for 15 seconds envision the speaker manifesting what she wants to manifest.

The person sitting to the left of the speaker is next and receives the share card. Similarly, the response card is passed on clock-wise. As described above, all participants receive an opportunity to speak and be supported.

Closing

When everyone has had a turn, the facilitator says: "Let's stand, form a circle and hold hands. Before we close with our affirmation, I would like to invite you to say in <u>one word</u> how you feel."

When everyone has had a turn, the meeting is closed with a group affirmation, "I am Spirit, You are Spirit, All is Spirit and All is Well."

Social

The host determines whether or not time is offered for socializing. If time is allowed for socializing, it is essential that people don't slide into complaining and blaming. Suggestion: instead of weekly socials, organize a social after the 12–week period and celebrate everyone's victories.

After the Meeting

The host, facilitator, and usher meet briefly after the meeting and make arrangements for the following week.

"Many thanks to Adrianus for being an organizer of a very powerful and intention filled group. I very much enjoyed meeting with you. I was greatly inspired by the wonderful intentions and emotions everyone shared. I now remind myself daily that I am spirit and all is well. Thank you for your inspiration."

- Tricia

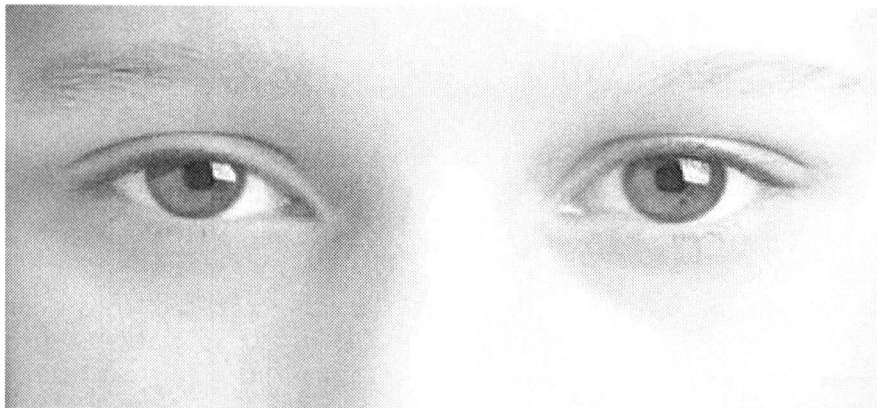

I am Spirit and so are You.

"I wasn't really sure what to expect when my doctor recommended I attend this workshop. I'm truly finding this to be a very wonderful experience! Thank you for welcoming me into the group with open arms! I felt very comfortable sharing how the past week was for me. The group is very supportive, and that is what I need, especially with all that is going on in my life. Thank you for doing this; it's truly amazing!"

- Heather

"Wonderful people who share a common sense of purpose and hopefulness."

- Joe

"I feel excited and joyful to be part of a spiritual group that supports integrity and authenticity."

- Zulma

Hosting a Meeting

Why would you want to host a meeting?

The first and foremost reason why you may want to host Spirits Onymous meetings is your passion for supporting the spiritual awakening in yourself and the people in your community. You have read the 12 principles and they strongly resonate with you. It's not necessary that you fully understand or even agree with them. But on an energetic level, you are attracted to what The InnerGuidance Network stands for. Additionally, you may want to:

- ❏ Meet like-minded people

- ❏ Attract people to your center, practice or service

- ❏ Make some extra money

Responsibilities of the host and facilitator

Find an appropriate place to offer the meetings, ideally a public place, such as a church, doctor's office, library, etc. Of course, you can offer a closed meeting for your friends and family in your living room, as well. Next, decide on a day and time for the meetings. Give yourself enough time to promote and launch the meetings. It is recommended that you start off with bi-weekly meetings and find at least one person to support you in the process.

Cost

Your expenses include renting the meeting space (or you may know an organization that is willing to donate a space to you). You are strongly encouraged to start a meetup-website: www.meetup.com. The cost for the meetup website varies from $12 to $19/month. Meetup offers easy tools to organize and promote your meeting.

Income

Enrollment fee for six bi-weekly meetings (1.5-2 hours each) may vary from location to location. It is best to go to the website to get the suggested fee: www.InnerGuidanceNetwork.org. The fee should cover all costs and reimburse the host for his or her time. Decide on a fee that covers the six meetings, including a Spirits Onymous Handbook. And decide on a fee per meeting for guests and for those who want to pay per meeting.

WE WANT YOU!

If you are interested in hosting and/or facilitating meetings go to The InnerGuidance Network website, click on "Spirits Onymous" and on "Hosting Spirits Onymous Meetings." Here you will find the latest information and the application form. After you have submitted the form, you will be contacted by email.

Listing on the InnerGuidance Network website

Your meeting will be officially registered after you have completed all your requirements and have submitted the details (date, time and location) of your meeting.

I am Spirit and so are You.

"Very interesting, thought provoking, even entertaining. The most important thing I got from the meetings is meeting other like-minded people. The other thing I really appreciated was sharing our experiences, so that we could help each other polish our techniques and raise our energies and vibrations. It can be so hard living in this human experience. It's very easy to get caught up in old thought patterns and habits, losing faith, and forgetting again all that we are, all that we are capable of."
- Sophia

"After one meeting, my opinion is that it appears to be a great group for enhancing one's ability to achieve one's life goals as well as for meeting friendly fellow sojourners."
- Jim

Chapter 5

THE INNERGUIDANCE NETWORK AND YOU

Becoming a member

All is Well

I trust that the truth of you being a spiritual entity having a human experience resonates deeply with you. It is your birthright to create a magnificent, meaningful and joyful existence. Beyond a shadow of a doubt, you have the innate wisdom to manifest your deepest desires. That's why you came into physical form. That's your purpose. And if you put your life in that perspective and encourage others to shape their lives in whatever way they feel inspired, a delicious existence for all is forthcoming.

But what has been preventing all the good people of the world to do that? The main reason is lack of focus. Most of us are distracted by drama and lose focus on what life is all about. Many of us have become addicted to adrenalin rushing through our arteries and the soap operas we entertain in our minds. Let's stop the drama! Right now. Let's kick the drama habit. Would you like to make a commitment to focus on who you truly are and create that magnificent life you intended to create? Would you?

Would you be willing to receive the support of other Spirits and in return support others on their journeys? If so, you may want to join The InnerGuidance Network. Within the network we remind each other of our true nature and our purpose during this lifetime. We see greatness in each other and encourage each other to stretch and shine.

You and I—unrelated to our social positions, race, nationalities and religions—need to step out of our semi-comfortable nooks and into the light. We owe it to ourselves and the rest of humanity to shed our facade and fulfill our roles as powerful creators. It behooves us to sustain and further build a network that supports us and sows seeds of consciousness into the world. Let's increase the vibrational energy and be the change we (wish to) see in the world.

The world needs leaders who lead by example, create mindfully, and touch the lives of people wherever they go. You are invited to fulfill such a role. You are invited to become a member of The InnerGuidance Network.

The InnerGuidance Network

Membership of the InnerGuidance Network

Instead of a membership fee, we ask you to purchase yearly three or more copies of the *Spirits Onymous Handbook* or *The ClearView Conspiracy* to give them as gifts. By doing this, you will invite family, friends, colleagues and perhaps utter strangers to let go of their attachment to drama and focus on the magnificence of life. You will be instrumental in helping them remember that indeed they are Spirit having a human experience. The books you distribute may remind them of their smoldering passion to create an extraordinary life.

In addition to giving away a thought-provoking read, the books invite readers to join a network of like-minded people, who support each other in manifesting meaningful and joy filled lives. Isn't that a nice gift to give?

Last, but not least, after gifting the books your conversations at the water cooler and at birthday parties may become a lot more interesting!

Becoming a member

Becoming a member is easy and it's free. Just go to The InnerGuidance Network website and register: www.InnerGuidanceNetwork.org.

Ordering copies

Order your three copies at the website or call your local meeting host.

Index of Tools

Each packets consists of:

Gratitude List

Transformation and Vision List

Dream Sheet

Collage Page

Quality of Life worksheet

Goal Plan 1

Goal Plan 2

My Bruises Sheet

Accomplishments Page

My Success Story

Chapter 6

TOOLS

Prompt Cards, Worksheets and more

We are Spiritual Beings having a Human Experience.

Facilitator's Prompt Card

Welcome to Spirits Onymous.

My name is _____, I am Spirit <u>and so are you.</u>

- ❏ Please take a minute and write on your gratitude list what you are grateful for. (1 min.)
- ❏ Now, go to the Transformation and Vision List and fill out this week's section: one minute. (1 min)
- ❏ Please, get comfortable, sit back and re—lax.
  CD: song, meditation and reading of the week – 12 min.

- ❏ Welcome. We are here to embrace our true nature. I am Spirit, You are Spirit, All is Spirit and All is Well.
- ❏ Participants of this meeting will maintain confidentiality and refrain from giving unsolicited advice.
- ❏ (Short announcements)
- ❏ (Re-read the bold text of the reading)
  Okay, let's take 15 minutes to discuss. How is this principle relevant to you? What came up during the reading? Who wants to start?
  Discussion: 15 min.

- ❏ The following 15 minutes, we'll take time for peer-coaching.
  (Direct the group to split up in peer-coaching pairs and ask them to work on:
  The Dream Sheet during meeting 1
  Quality of Life Sheet, column 1, during meeting 2
  Quality of Life Sheet, column 2 and 3, during meeting 3
  Goal Sheet during meeting 4
  Goal Sheet during meeting 5
  Accomplishments Page during meeting 6
  When new people are present, discuss the basic format for peer-coaching, see page 97)

  Peer-Coaching: 15 min.

❑ Okay, let's come back in the group and do the Transformation and Vision Sequence.

CD: Transformation and Vision Sequence - 7 min.

❑ Each of us has approximately _____ minutes to share.

See allotted sharing time on timetable below - 35 min.

❑ Let's hold hands. Before we close with our affirmation, I would like to invite you to say in <u>one word</u> how you feel.

❑ <u>Together</u>: I am Spirit, You are Spirit, All is Spirit and All is Well.

Sharing time schedule

Based on ± 35 minutes sharing time.

Participants	Sharing time per person (+30 sec response)
6	5 min, 20 sec
7	4 min, 30 sec
8	4 min
9	3 min
10	3 min
11	2 min, 40 sec
12	2 min, 30 sec
13	same
14	same

When 14 or more participants: split in 2 groups.

When 30 or more: split in 3 groups.

When 40 or more: split in 4 groups.

Hello, my name is _____, I am Spirit.

Take a deep breath as you decide what you want to share:

A gratitude

This week's reading

How a challenging situation helped you grow spiritually

What would you like to manifest next week?

_____, we unconditionally

name

love and support you.

You are a wise and powerful creator.

You are Spirit and All is Well.

My Great Moments List

Close your eyes and picture your life. Write down five to ten moments or phases in your life when you felt ecstatic, passionate or profoundly happy?

Look over the list. What patterns do you notice? Why were these moments so enjoyable?

WINTER 2007-2008
TOOL PACKET

Gratitude List

Transformation and Vision List

Dream Sheet

Collage Page

Quality of Life worksheet

Goal Plan 1

Goal Plan 2

My Bruises Sheet

Accomplishments Page

My Success Story

GRATITUDE LIST
SPIRITS ONYMOUS WINTER SESSION 2007-2008

Take a deep breath and look back at the last seven days: what are you grateful for? What did you accomplish?

Week of:	
Dec 9 Step 1	
Dec 16 Step 2	
Dec 23 Step 3	
Dec 30 Step 4	
Jan 6, 2008 Step 5	
Jan 13 Step 6	

Jan 20 Step 7	
Jan 27 Step 8	
Feb 3 Step 9	
Feb 10 Step 10	
Feb 17 Step 11	
Feb 24 Step 12	

Notes:

TRANSFORMATION AND VISION LIST
SPIRITS ONYMOUS WINTER SESSION 2007-2008

(**A**): Write down the most upsetting emotion you experienced during the last week, e.g. anger. (**B**): On a scale of 1 to 10, how troubling was it or is it? (**C**): Are you willing to take full responsibility and explore what the emotion is trying to tell you? (**D**): Listen to the Transformation and Vision Sequence (audio program on Spirits Onymous E-campus) and write down the vision you would like to hold this week. Write it in the present tense and positively, e.g. "I'm having a loving relationship. (**E**): Write down the names of the person(s) you will approach this week with the intention to see their greatness and express that to them. Start with friends, family and colleagues. The People don't need to be different every week. Remember: **HAVE FUN!**

2008 Week of:	(A): *Anger* , (B): *8* , (C) *Yes* (D): *I'm having a loving relationship with my partner*.	(E) *Mary* *Dad*
Dec 9 Step 1	——————————, ————, *Yes / No / Not Yet*	———
Dec 16 Step 2	——————————, ————, *Yes / No / Not Yet*	———
Dec 23 Step 3	——————————, ————, *Yes / No / Not Yet*	———
Dec 30 Step 4	——————————, ————, *Yes / No / Not Yet*	———
Jan 6, 2008 Step 5	——————————, ————, *Yes / No / Not Yet*	———

Jan 13 Step 6	——————————, ————,	*Yes / No / Not Yet*	————
Jan 20 Step 7	——————————, ————,	*Yes / No / Not Yet*	————
Jan 27 Step 8	——————————, ————,	*Yes / No / Not Yet*	————
Feb 3 Step 9	——————————, ————,	*Yes / No / Not Yet*	————
Feb 10 Step 10	——————————, ————,	*Yes / No / Not Yet*	————
Feb 17 Step 11	——————————, ————,	*Yes / No / Not Yet*	————
Feb 24 Step 12	——————————, ————,	*Yes / No / Not Yet*	————

This form can be downloaded as a PDF file at www.InnerGuidanceNetwork.org:
Spirits Onymous Campus: membership store: free stuff.

Copyright © 2005-2008, Adrianus Van Munster, All Rights Reserved

DREAM SHEET

If you had a magic wand, what kind of future would you create? Imagine that virtually everything is possible. Dream away! Describe the images that come up:

COLLAGE

SPIRITS ONYMOUS WINTER SESSION 2007-2008

QUALITY OF LIFE

SPIRITS ONYMOUS WINTER SESSION 2007-2008

Column 1

Areas	Per area, describe your ideal future in 2 to 5 words. *Dream away, the sky is the limit.*
Health	
Work	
Family	
Romance	
Friendship	
Finances	
Knowledge	
Home	
Spirituality	
Recreation	
Community	
My Legacy	

Fill out this form in three steps. First fill out column 1.
Next, preferably a couple of days later, column 2.
Lastly, indicate your priority in column 3.

Areas	Column 2 Specific goals reached <u>within 3 months</u>	Column 3 Priority
Health		
Work		
Family		
Romance		
Friendship		
Finances		
Knowledge		
Home		
Spirituality		
Recreation		
Community		
My Legacy		

GOAL: _____

Today's date: _____

Date you want this goal to be accomplished: _____

A. Imagine that you already have reached your goal and describe—*in the present time*—what you see, hear and especially *feel.* Be specific:

B. At least twice a day, take five to ten minutes to daydream and imagine that you already have reached the goal & *feel good about it*.

C. Design a five-step goal plan toward your goal, but <u>only</u> fill out the first two steps. When you have reached the first two steps, decide on your next step. Review your goal plan daily. Make it a top priority.

D. Expect that you will reach your goal effortlessly.

E. Before going to sleep, release, and trust that the Universe will take care of the details.

STEP 1.

_____

Date step 1 accomplished: _____

STEP 2.

_____

Date step 2 accomplished: _____

STEP 3.

_____

Date step 3 accomplished: _____

STEP 4.

_____

Date step 4 accomplished: _____

STEP 5.

_____

Date step 5 accomplished: _____

<u>Comments:</u>

This form can be downloaded as a PDF file at www.InnerGuidanceNetwork.org:
Spirits Onymous Campus: membership store: free stuff.

GOAL PLAN 2

GOAL: _____

Today's date: _____

Date you want this goal to be accomplished: _____

A.   Imagine that you already have reached your goal and describe—*in the present time*—what you see, hear and especially *feel.* Be specific:

B.   At least twice a day, take five to ten minutes to daydream and imagine that you already have reached the goal & *feel good about it*.

C. Design a five-step goal plan toward your goal, but <u>only</u> fill out the first two steps. When you have reached the first two steps, decide on your next step. Review your goal plan daily. Make it a top priority.

D. Expect that you will reach your goal effortlessly.

E. Before going to sleep, release, and trust that the Universe will take care of the details.

STEP 1.

_____

Date step 1 accomplished: _____

STEP 2.

_____

Date step 2 accomplished: _____

STEP 3.

_____

Date step 3 accomplished: _____

STEP 4.

_____

Date step 4 accomplished: _____

STEP 5.

_____

Date step 5 accomplished: _____

<u>Comments:</u>

This form can be downloaded as a PDF file at www.InnerGuidanceNetwork.org: Spirits Onymous Campus: membership store: free stuff.

MY BRUISES

Review your life and identify situations or behaviors that tend to trigger you and get you upset. Resist the tendency to analyze your "issues," blame others or yourself. Just make a list:

1. Choose the most current and most upsetting situation and acknowledge the emotion (anger, sadness, etc,) that was triggered. Describe the emotion:

2. Hold it and give it love for as long as you need to. Breathe through the pain.

3. After some time, slowly turn "your boat" around. Consider the pain a Cosmic wakeup call. What is it asking you to do? Ask yourself how you would like to feel, imagine what that would look like, and gently float into that direction. Realize that only *you* can push the rudder around. Loosen your grip and give birth to a new reality. Fill your mind and heart with what you want to manifest and ***smile***.

Do you need a therapist or counselor?
If it is really hard to let go of your anger or sadness, you may want to reach out and get professional support. A word of caution: before you decide on a therapist or counselor, interview him or her first! You want to work with a therapist who is skilled in assisting you to take full responsibility, help you learn from the situation and move through it. When in doubt, you may contact an InnerGuidance Network coach who can assist you in this process.

This form can be downloaded as a PDF file at www.InnerGuidanceNetwork.org:
Spirits Onymous Campus: membership store: free stuff.

ACCOMPLISHMENTS PAGE

SPIRITS ONYMOUS WINTER SESSION 2007-2008

MY SUCCESS STORY
SPIRITS ONYMOUS WINTER SESSION 2007-2008

We would love to see your story!

For more information, go to www.InnerGuidanceNetwork.org, click on "Spirits Onymous" and look for "Submit Your Success Story." Your story may end up on the website and in next year's handbook.

SPRING 2008
TOOL PACKET

Gratitude List

Transformation and Vision List

Dream Sheet

Collage Page

Quality of Life worksheet

Goal Plan 1

Goal Plan 2

My Bruises Sheet

Accomplishments Page

My Success Story

GRATITUDE LIST
SPIRITS ONYMOUS SPRING SESSION 2008

Take a deep breath and look back at the last seven days: what are you grateful for? What did you accomplish?

Week of:	
March 9 Step 1	
March 16 Step 2	
March 23 Step 3	
March 30 Step 4	
April 6 Step 5	
April 13 Step 6	

April 20 Step 7	
April 27 Step 8	
May 4 Step 9	
May 11 Step 10	
May 18 Step 11	
May 25 Step 12	

Notes:

This form can be downloaded as a PDF file at www.InnerGuidanceNetwork.org:
Spirits Onymous Campus: membership store: free stuff.

TRANSFORMATION AND VISION LIST

SPIRITS ONYMOUS SPRING SESSION 2008

(**A**): Write down the most upsetting emotion you experienced during the last week, e.g. anger. (**B**): On a scale of 1 to 10, how troubling was it or is it? (**C**): Are you willing to take full responsibility and explore what the emotion is trying to tell you? (**D**): Listen to the Transformation and Vision Sequence (audio program on Spirits Onymous E-campus) and write down the vision you would like to hold this week. Write it in the present tense and positively, e.g. "I'm having a loving relationship. (**E**): Write down the names of the person(s) you will approach this week with the intention to see their greatness and express that to them. Start with friends, family and colleagues. The people don't need to be different every week. Remember: **HAVE FUN!**

2008 Week of:	(A): *Anger* , (B): *8* , (C) *Yes* (D): *I'm having a loving relationship with my partner*.	(E) *Mary* *Dad*
March 9 Step 1	_____ , _____ , *Yes / No / Not Yet*	____
March 16 Step 2	_____ , _____ , *Yes / No / Not Yet*	____
March 23 Step 3	_____ , _____ , *Yes / No / Not Yet*	____
March 30 Step 4	_____ , _____ , *Yes / No / Not Yet*	____
April 6 Step 5	_____ , _____ , *Yes / No / Not Yet*	____

April 13 Step 6	_____, _____,	*Yes / No / Not Yet*	____
April 20 Step 7	_____, _____,	*Yes / No / Not Yet*	____
April 27 Step 8	_____, _____,	*Yes / No / Not Yet*	____
May 4 Step 9	_____, _____,	*Yes / No / Not Yet*	____
May 11 Step 10	_____, _____,	*Yes / No / Not Yet*	____
May 18 Step 11	_____, _____,	*Yes / No / Not Yet*	____
May 25 Step 12	_____, _____,	*Yes / No / Not Yet*	____

This form can be downloaded as a PDF file at www.InnerGuidanceNetwork.org:
Spirits Onymous Campus: membership store: free stuff.

DREAM SHEET

SPIRITS ONYMOUS SPRING SESSION 2008

If you had a magic wand, what kind of future would you create?
Imagine that virtually everything is possible. Dream away! Describe the
images that come up:

COLLAGE

SPIRITS ONYMOUS SPRING SESSION 2008

QUALITY OF LIFE

SPIRITS ONYMOUS SPRING SESSION 2008

Column 1

Areas	Per area, describe your ideal future in 2 to 5 words. *Dream away, the sky is the limit.*
Health	
Work	
Family	
Romance	
Friendship	
Finances	
Knowledge	
Home	
Spirituality	
Recreation	
Community	
My Legacy	

Fill out this form in three steps. First fill out column 1.
Next, preferably a couple of days later, column 2.
Lastly, indicate your priority in column 3.

Areas	Column 2 Specific goals reached <u>within 3 months</u>	Column 3 Priority
Health		
Work		
Family		
Romance		
Friendship		
Finances		
Knowledge		
Home		
Spirituality		
Recreation		
Community		
My Legacy		

GOAL: _____

Today's date: _____

Date you want this goal to be accomplished: _____

A. Imagine that you already have reached your goal and describe—*in the present time*—what you see, hear and especially *feel.* Be specific:

B. At least twice a day, take five to ten minutes to daydream and imagine that you already have reached the goal & *feel good about it.*

C. Design a five-step goal plan toward your goal, but <u>only</u> fill out the first two steps. When you have reached the first two steps, decide on your next step. Review your goal plan daily. Make it a top priority.

D. Expect that you will reach your goal effortlessly.

E. Before going to sleep, release, and trust that the Universe will take care of the details.

STEP 1.

_____

Date step 1 accomplished: _____

STEP 2.

_____

Date step 2 accomplished: _____

STEP 3.

_____

Date step 3 accomplished: _____

STEP 4.

_____

Date step 4 accomplished: _____

STEP 5.

_____

Date step 5 accomplished: _____

Comments:

GOAL: _____

Today's date: _____

Date you want this goal to be accomplished: _____

A. Imagine that you already have reached your goal and describe—*in the present time*—what you see, hear and especially *feel.* Be specific:

B. At least twice a day, take five to ten minutes to daydream and imagine that you already have reached the goal & *feel good about it*.

C. Design a five-step goal plan toward your goal, but <u>only</u> fill out the first two steps. When you have reached the first two steps, decide on your next step. Review your goal plan daily. Make it a top priority.

D. Expect that you will reach your goal effortlessly.

E. Before going to sleep, release, and trust that the Universe will take care of the details.

STEP 1.

_____

Date step 1 accomplished: _____

STEP 2.

_____

Date step 2 accomplished: _____

STEP 3.

_____

Date step 3 accomplished: _____

STEP 4.

_____

Date step 4 accomplished: _____

STEP 5.

_____

Date step 5 accomplished: _____

Comments:

This form can be downloaded as a PDF file at www.InnerGuidanceNetwork.org: Spirits Onymous Campus: membership store: free stuff.

MY BRUISES

Review your life and identify situations or behaviors that tend to trigger you and get you upset. Resist the tendency to analyze your "issues," blame others or yourself. Just make a list:

1. Choose the most current and most upsetting situation and acknowledge the emotion (anger, sadness, etc,) that was triggered. Describe the emotion:

2. Hold it and give it love for as long as you need to. Breathe through the pain.

3. After some time, slowly turn "your boat" around. Consider the pain a Cosmic wakeup call. What is it asking you to do? Ask yourself how you would like to feel, imagine what that would look like, and gently float into that direction. Realize that only *you* can push the rudder around. Loosen your grip and give birth to a new reality. Fill your mind and heart with what you want to manifest and *smile*.

Do you need a therapist or counselor?
If it is really hard to let go of your anger or sadness, you may want to reach out and get professional support. A word of caution: before you decide on a therapist or counselor, interview him or her first! You want to work with a therapist who is skilled in assisting you to take full responsibility, help you learn from the situation and move through it. When in doubt, you may contact an InnerGuidance Network coach who can assist you in this process.

This form can be downloaded as a PDF file at www.InnerGuidanceNetwork.org:
Spirits Onymous Campus: membership store: free stuff.

ACCOMPLISHMENTS PAGE
SPIRITS ONYMOUS SPRING SESSION 2008

MY SUCCESS STORY

SPIRITS ONYMOUS SPRING SESSION 2008

We would love to see your story!

For more information, go to www.InnerGuidanceNetwork.org, click on "Spirits Onymous" and look for "Submit Your Success Story." Your story may end up on the website and in next year's handbook.

SUMMER 2008
TOOL PACKET

Gratitude List

Transformation and Vision List

Dream Sheet

Collage Page

Quality of Life worksheet

Goal Plan 1

Goal Plan 2

My Bruises Sheet

Accomplishments Page

My Success Story

GRATITUDE LIST
SPIRITS ONYMOUS SUMMER SESSION 2008

Take a deep breath and look back at the last seven days: what are you grateful for? What did you accomplish?

Week of:	
June 8 Step 1	
June 15 Step 2	
June 22 Step 3	
June 29 Step 4	
July 6 Step 5	
July 13 Step 6	

July 20 Step 7	
July 27 Step 8	
Aug 3 Step 9	
Aug 10 Step 10	
Aug 17 Step 11	
Aug 24 Step 12	

Notes:

TRANSFORMATION AND VISION LIST
SPIRITS ONYMOUS SUMMER SESSION 2008

(**A**): Write down the most upsetting emotion you experienced during the last week, e.g. anger. (**B**): On a scale of 1 to 10, how troubling was it or is it? (**C**): Are you willing to take full responsibility and explore what the emotion is trying to tell you? (**D**): Listen to the Transformation and Vision Sequence (audio program on Spirits Onymous E-campus) and write down the vision you would like to hold this week. Write it in the present tense and positively, e.g. "I'm having a loving relationship. (**E**): Write down the names of the person(s) you will approach this week with the intention to see their greatness and express that to them. Start with friends, family and colleagues. The people don't need to be different every week. Remember: **HAVE FUN!**

2008 Week of:	(A): *Anger* , (B): *8* , (C) *Yes* (D): *I'm having a loving relationship with my partner.*	(E) *Mary* *Dad*
June 8 Step 1	—————————, ————, *Yes / No / Not Yet*	————
June 15 Step 2	—————————, ————, *Yes / No / Not Yet*	————
June 22 Step 3	—————————, ————, *Yes / No / Not Yet*	————
June 29 Step 4	—————————, ————, *Yes / No / Not Yet*	————
July 6 Step 5	—————————, ————, *Yes / No / Not Yet*	————

July 13 Step 6	—————————, ———, *Yes / No / Not Yet*	———
July 20 Step 7	—————————, ———, *Yes / No / Not Yet*	———
July 27 Step 8	—————————, ———, *Yes / No / Not Yet*	———
Aug 3 Step 9	—————————, ———, *Yes / No / Not Yet*	———
Aug 10 Step 10	—————————, ———, *Yes / No / Not Yet*	———
Aug 17 Step 11	—————————, ———, *Yes / No / Not Yet*	———
Aug 24 Step 12	—————————, ———, *Yes / No / Not Yet*	———

This form can be downloaded as a PDF file at www.InnerGuidanceNetwork.org:
Spirits Onymous Campus: membership store: free stuff.

DREAM SHEET

If you had a magic wand, what kind of future would you create? Imagine that virtually everything is possible. Dream away! Describe the images that come up:

COLLAGE

SPIRITS ONYMOUS SUMMER SESSION 2008

QUALITY OF LIFE

SPIRITS ONYMOUS SUMMER SESSION 2008

Column 1

Area	Per area, describe your ideal future in 2 to 5 words. *Dream away, the sky is the limit.*
Health	
Work	
Family	
Romance	
Friendship	
Finances	
Knowledge	
Home	
Spirituality	
Recreation	
Community	
My Legacy	

Fill out this form in three steps. First fill out column 1.
Next, preferably a couple of days later, column 2.
Lastly, indicate your priority in column 3.

Areas	Column 2 — Specific goals reached <u>within 3 months</u>	Column 3 — Priority
Health		
Work		
Family		
Romance		
Friendship		
Finances		
Knowledge		
Home		
Spirituality		
Recreation		
Community		
My Legacy		

GOAL: _____

Today's date: _____

Date you want this goal to be accomplished: _____

A. Imagine that you already have reached your goal and describe—*in the present time*—what you see, hear and especially *feel.* Be specific:

B. At least twice a day, take five to ten minutes to daydream and imagine that you already have reached the goal & *feel good about it.*

C. Design a five-step goal plan toward your goal, but <u>only</u> fill out the first two steps. When you have reached the first two steps, decide on your next step. Review your goal plan daily. Make it a top priority.

D. Expect that you will reach your goal effortlessly.

E. Before going to sleep, release, and trust that the Universe will take care of the details.

STEP 1.

_____

Date step 1 accomplished: _____

STEP 2.

_____

Date step 2 accomplished: _____

STEP 3.

_____

Date step 3 accomplished: _____

STEP 4.

_____

Date step 4 accomplished: _____

STEP 5.

_____

Date step 5 accomplished: _____

<u>Comments:</u>

GOAL: _____

Today's date: _____

Date you want this goal to be accomplished: _____

A.   Imagine that you already have reached your goal and describe—*in the present time*—what you see, hear and especially *feel.* Be specific:

B.   At least twice a day, take five to ten minutes to daydream and imagine that you already have reached the goal & *feel good about it*.

C. Design a five-step goal plan toward your goal, but <u>only</u> fill out the first two steps. When you have reached the first two steps, decide on your next step. Review your goal plan daily. Make it a top priority.

D. Expect that you will reach your goal effortlessly.

E. Before going to sleep, release, and trust that the Universe will take care of the details.

STEP 1.

_____

Date step 1 accomplished: _____

STEP 2.

_____

Date step 2 accomplished: _____

STEP 3.

_____

Date step 3 accomplished: _____

STEP 4.

_____

Date step 4 accomplished: _____

STEP 5.

_____

Date step 5 accomplished: _____

Comments:

MY BRUISES

Review your life and identify situations or behaviors that tend to trigger you and get you upset. Resist the tendency to analyze your "issues," blame others or yourself. Just make a list:

1. Choose the most current and most upsetting situation and acknowledge the emotion (anger, sadness, etc,) that was triggered. Describe the emotion:

2. Hold it and give it love for as long as you need to. Breathe through the pain.

3. After some time, slowly turn "your boat" around. Consider the pain a Cosmic wakeup call. What is it asking you to do? Ask yourself how you would like to feel, imagine what that would look like, and gently float into that direction. Realize that only *you* can push the rudder around. Loosen your grip and give birth to a new reality. Fill your mind and heart with what you want to manifest and ***smile***.

Do you need a therapist or counselor?
If it is really hard to let go of your anger or sadness, you may want to reach out and get professional support. A word of caution: before you decide on a therapist or counselor, interview him or her first! You want to work with a therapist who is skilled in assisting you to take full responsibility, help you learn from the situation and move through it. When in doubt, you may contact an InnerGuidance Network coach who can assist you in this process.

This form can be downloaded as a PDF file at www.InnerGuidanceNetwork.org:
Spirits Onymous Campus: membership store: free stuff.

ACCOMPLISHMENTS PAGE

SPIRITS ONYMOUS SUMMER SESSION 2008

SUCCESS STORY
SPIRITS ONYMOUS SUMMER SESSION 2008

We would love to see your story!

For more information, go to www.InnerGuidanceNetwork.org, click on "Spirits Onymous" and look for "Submit Your Success Story." Your story may end up on the website and in next year's handbook.

FALL 2008
TOOL PACKET

Gratitude List

Transformation and Vision List

Dream Sheet

Collage Page

Quality of Life worksheet

Goal Plan 1

Goal Plan 2

My Bruises Sheet

Accomplishments Page

My Success Story

GRATITUDE LIST
SPIRITS ONYMOUS FALL SESSION 2008

Take a deep breath and look back at the last seven days: what are you grateful for? What did you accomplish?

Week of:	
Sept 7 Step 1	
Sept 14 Step 2	
Sept 21 Step 3	
Sept 28 Step 4	
Oct 5 Step 5	
Oct 12 Step 6	

Oct 19 Step 7	
Oct 26 Step 8	
Nov 2 Step 9	
Nov 9 Step 10	
Nov 16 Step 11	
Nov 23 Step 12	

Notes:

This form can be downloaded as a PDF file at www.InnerGuidanceNetwork.org:
Spirits Onymous Campus: membership store: free stuff.

TRANSFORMATION AND VISION LIST
SPIRITS ONYMOUS FALL SESSION 2008

(**A**): Write down the most upsetting emotion you experienced during the last week, e.g. anger. (**B**): On a scale of 1 to 10, how troubling was it or is it? (**C**): Are you willing to take full responsibility and explore what the emotion is trying to tell you? (**D**): Listen to the Transformation and Vision Sequence (audio program on Spirits Onymous E-campus) and write down the vision you would like to hold this week. Write it in the present tense and positively, e.g. "I'm having a loving relationship. (**E**): Write down the names of the person(s) you will approach this week with the intention to see their greatness and express that to them. Start with friends, family and colleagues. The people don't need to be different every week. Remember: **HAVE FUN!**

2008 Week of:	(A): *Anger* , (B): *8* , (C) *Yes* (D): *I'm having a loving relationship with my partner.*	(E) *Mary* *Dad*
Sept 7 Step 1	—————————, ———, *Yes / No / Not Yet*	———
Sept 14 Step 2	—————————, ———, *Yes / No / Not Yet*	———
Sept 21 Step 3	—————————, ———, *Yes / No / Not Yet*	———
Sept 28 Step 4	—————————, ———, *Yes / No / Not Yet*	———
Oct 5 Step 5	—————————, ———, *Yes / No / Not Yet*	———

Oct 12 Step 6	————————————, ————,	*Yes / No / Not Yet*	————
Oct 19 Step 7	————————————, ————,	*Yes / No / Not Yet*	————
Oct 26 Step 8	————————————, ————,	*Yes / No / Not Yet*	————
Nov 2 Step 9	————————————, ————,	*Yes / No / Not Yet*	————
Nov 9 Step 10	————————————, ————,	*Yes / No / Not Yet*	————
Nov 16 Step 11	————————————, ————,	*Yes / No / Not Yet*	————
Nov 23 Step 12	————————————, ————,	*Yes / No / Not Yet*	————

This form can be downloaded as a PDF file at www.InnerGuidanceNetwork.org:
Spirits Onymous Campus: membership store: free stuff.

DREAM SHEET

If you had a magic wand, what kind of future would you create? Imagine that virtually everything is possible. Dream away! Describe the images that come up:

COLLAGE

SPIRITS ONYMOUS FALL SESSION 2008

QUALITY OF LIFE

SPIRITS ONYMOUS FALL SESSION 2008

Column 1

Areas	Per area, describe your ideal future in 2 to 5 words. *Dream away, the sky is the limit.*
Health	
Work	
Family	
Romance	
Friendship	
Finances	
Knowledge	
Home	
Spirituality	
Recreation	
Community	
My Legacy	

Fill out this form in three steps. First fill out column 1.
Next, preferably a couple of days later, column 2.
Lastly, indicate your priority in column 3.

Areas	Column 2 Specific goals reached <u>within 3 months</u>	Column 3 Priority
Health		
Work		
Family		
Romance		
Friendship		
Finances		
Knowledge		
Home		
Spirituality		
Recreation		
Community		
My Legacy		

GOAL: _____

Today's date: _____

Date you want this goal to be accomplished: _____

A. Imagine that you already have reached your goal and describe—*in the present time*—what you see, hear and especially *feel.* Be specific:

B. At least twice a day, take five to ten minutes to daydream and imagine that you already have reached the goal & *feel good about it*.

C. Design a five-step goal plan toward your goal, but <u>only</u> fill out the first two steps. When you have reached the first two steps, decide on your next step. Review your goal plan daily. Make it a top priority.

D. Expect that you will reach your goal effortlessly.

E. Before you go to sleep, release, and trust that the Universe will take care of the details.

STEP 1.

_____

Date step 1 accomplished: _____

STEP 2.

_____

Date step 2 accomplished: _____

STEP 3.

_____

Date step 3 accomplished: _____

STEP 4.

_____

Date step 4 accomplished: _____

STEP 5.

_____

Date step 5 accomplished: _____

<u>Comments:</u>

GOAL: _____

Today's date: _____

Date you want this goal to be accomplished: _____

A. Imagine that you already have reached your goal and describe—*in the present time*—what you see, hear and especially *feel.* Be specific:

B. At least twice a day, take five to ten minutes to daydream and imagine that you already have reached the goal & *feel good about it.*

C. Design a five-step goal plan toward your goal, but <u>only</u> fill out the first two steps. When you have reached the first two steps, decide on your next step. Review your goal plan daily. Make it a top priority.

D. Expect that you will reach your goal effortlessly.

E. Before you go to sleep, release, and trust that the Universe will take care of the details.

STEP 1.

_____

Date step 1 accomplished: _____

STEP 2.

_____

Date step 2 accomplished: _____

STEP 3.

_____

Date step 3 accomplished: _____

STEP 4.

_____

Date step 4 accomplished: _____

STEP 5.

_____

Date step 5 accomplished: _____

Comments:

This form can be downloaded as a PDF file at www.InnerGuidanceNetwork.org: Spirits Onymous Campus: membership store: free stuff.

MY BRUISES

Review your life and identify situations or behaviors that tend to trigger you and get you upset. Resist the tendency to analyze your "issues," blame others or yourself. Just make a list:

✗

✗

✗

1. Choose the most current and most upsetting situation and acknowledge the emotion (anger, sadness, etc,) that was triggered. Describe the emotion:

2. Hold it and give it love for as long as you need to. Breathe through the pain.

3. After some time, slowly turn "your boat" around. Consider the pain a Cosmic wakeup call. What is it asking you to do? Ask yourself how you would like to feel, imagine what that would look like, and gently float into that direction. Realize that only *you* can push the rudder around. Loosen your grip and give birth to a new reality. Fill your mind and heart with what you want to manifest and ***smile***.

Do you need a therapist or counselor?
If it is really hard to let go of your anger or sadness, you may want to reach out and get professional support. A word of caution: before you decide on a therapist or counselor, interview him or her first! You want to work with a therapist who is skilled in assisting you to take full responsibility, help you learn from the situation and move through it. When in doubt, you may contact an InnerGuidance Network coach who can assist you in this process.

This form can be downloaded as a PDF file at www.InnerGuidanceNetwork.org: Spirits Onymous Campus: membership store: free stuff.

ACCOMPLISHMENTS PAGE

SPIRITS ONYMOUS FALL SESSION 2008

SUCCESS STORY

SPIRITS ONYMOUS FALL SESSION 2008

We would love to see your story!

For more information, go to www.InnerGuidanceNetwork.org, click on "Spirits Onymous" and look for "Submit Your Success Story." Your story may end up on the website and in next year's handbook.

WINTER 2008 - 2009
TOOL PACKET

Gratitude List

Transformation and Vision List

Dream Sheet

Collage Page

Quality of Life worksheet

Goal Plan 1

Goal Plan 2

My Bruises Sheet

Accomplishments Page

My Success Story

GRATITUDE LIST
SPIRITS ONYMOUS WINTER SESSION 2008-2009

Take a deep breath and look back at the last seven days: what are you grateful for? What did you accomplish?

Week of:	
Dec 7 Step 1	
Dec 14 Step 2	
Dec 21 Step 3	
Dec 28 Step 4	
Jan 4, 2009 Step 5	
Jan 11 Step 6	

Jan 18 Step 7	
Jan 25 Step 8	
Feb 1 Step 9	
Feb 8 Step 10	
Feb 15 Step 11	
Feb 22 Step 17	

Notes:

This form can be downloaded as a PDF file at www.InnerGuidanceNetwork.org:
Spirits Onymous Campus: membership store: free stuff.

TRANSFORMATION AND VISION LIST
SPIRITS ONYMOUS WINTER SESSION 2008-2009

(**A**): Write down the most upsetting emotion you experienced during the last week, e.g. anger. (**B**): On a scale of 1 to 10, how troubling was it or is it? (**C**): Are you willing to take full responsibility and explore what the emotion is trying to tell you? (**D**): Listen to the Transformation and Vision Sequence (audio program on Spirits Onymous E-campus) and write down the vision you would like to hold this week. Write it in the present tense and positively, e.g. "I'm having a loving relationship. (**E**): Write down the names of the person(s) you will approach this week with the intention to see their greatness and express that to them. Start with friends, family and colleagues. The people don't need to be different every week. Remember: **HAVE FUN!**

2008 Week of:	(A): *Anger* , (B): *8* , (C) *Yes* (D): *I'm having a loving relationship with my partner.*	(E) *Mary* *Dad*
Dec 7 Step 1	——————, ———, *Yes / No / Not Yet*	———
Dec 14 Step 2	——————, ———, *Yes / No / Not Yet*	———
Dec 21 Step 3	——————, ———, *Yes / No / Not Yet*	———
Dec 28 Step 4	——————, ———, *Yes / No / Not Yet*	———
Jan 4, 2009 Step 5	——————, ———, *Yes / No / Not Yet*	———

Jan 11 Step 6	————————, ———, *Yes / No / Not Yet*	———
Jan 18 Step 7	————————, ———, *Yes / No / Not Yet*	———
Jan 25 Step 8	————————, ———, *Yes / No / Not Yet*	———
Feb 1 Step 9	————————, ———, *Yes / No / Not Yet*	———
Feb 8 Step 10	————————, ———, *Yes / No / Not Yet*	———
Feb 15 Step 11	————————, ———, *Yes / No / Not Yet*	———
Feb 22 Step 17	————————, ———, *Yes / No / Not Yet*	———

DREAM SHEET

If you had a magic wand, what kind of future would you create? Imagine that virtually everything is possible. Dream away! Describe the images that come up:

COLLAGE

SPIRITS ONYMOUS WINTER SESSION 2008-2009

QUALITY OF LIFE

Column 1

Areas	Per area, describe your ideal future in 2 to 5 words. *Dream away, the sky is the limit.*
Health	
Work	
Family	
Romance	
Friendship	
Finances	
Knowledge	
Home	
Spirituality	
Recreation	
Community	
My Legacy	

Fill out this form in three steps. First fill out column 1.
Next, preferably a couple of days later, column 2.
Lastly, indicate your priority in column 3.

	Column 2	Column 3
Areas	**Specific goals reached <u>within 3 months</u>**	**Priority**
Health		
Work		
Family		
Romance		
Friendship		
Finances		
Knowledge		
Home		
Spirituality		
Recreation		
Community		
My Legacy		

GOAL: _____

Today's date: _____

Date you want this goal to be accomplished: _____

A. Imagine that you already have reached your goal and describe—*in the present time*—what you see, hear and especially *feel.* Be specific:

B. At least twice a day, take five to ten minutes to daydream and imagine that you already have reached the goal & *feel good about it*.

C. Design a five-step goal plan toward your goal, but <u>only</u> fill out the first two steps. When you have reached the first two steps, decide on your next step. Review your goal plan daily. Make it a top priority.

D. Expect that you will reach your goal effortlessly.

E. Before you go to sleep, release, and trust that the Universe will take care of the details.

STEP 1.

_____

Date step 1 accomplished: _____

STEP 2.

_____

Date step 2 accomplished: _____

STEP 3.

_____

Date step 3 accomplished: _____

STEP 4.

_____

Date step 4 accomplished: _____

STEP 5.

_____

Date step 5 accomplished: _____

Comments:

GOAL: _____

Today's date: _____

Date you want this goal to be accomplished: _____

A. Imagine that you already have reached your goal and describe—*in the present time*—what you see, hear and especially *feel.* Be specific:

B. At least twice a day, take five to ten minutes to daydream and imagine that you already have reached the goal & *feel good about it*.

C. Design a five-step goal plan toward your goal, but <u>only</u> fill out the first two steps. When you have reached the first two steps, decide on your next step. Review your goal plan daily. Make it a top priority.

D. Expect that you will reach your goal effortlessly.

E. Before you go to sleep, release, and trust that the Universe will take care of the details.

STEP 1.

_____

Date step 1 accomplished: _____

STEP 2.

_____

Date step 2 accomplished: _____

STEP 3.

_____

Date step 3 accomplished: _____

STEP 4.

_____

Date step 4 accomplished: _____

STEP 5.

_____

Date step 5 accomplished: _____

Comments:

This form can be downloaded as a PDF file at www.InnerGuidanceNetwork.org: Spirits Onymous Campus: membership store: free stuff.

MY BRUISES

Review your life and identify situations or behaviors that tend to trigger you and get you upset. Resist the tendency to analyze your "issues," blame others or yourself. Just make a list:

1. Choose the most current and most upsetting situation and acknowledge the emotion (anger, sadness, etc,) that was triggered. Describe the emotion:

2. Hold it and give it love for as long as you need to. Breathe through the pain.

3. After some time, slowly turn "your boat" around. Consider the pain a Cosmic wakeup call. What is it asking you to do? Ask yourself how you would like to feel, imagine what that would look like, and gently float into that direction. Realize that only *you* can push the rudder around. Loosen your grip and give birth to a new reality. Fill your mind and heart with what you want to manifest and ***smile***.

Do you need a therapist or counselor?

If it is really hard to let go of your anger or sadness, you may want to reach out and get professional support. A word of caution: before you decide on a therapist or counselor, interview him or her first! You want to work with a therapist who is skilled in assisting you to take full responsibility, help you learn from the situation and move through it. When in doubt, you may contact an InnerGuidance Network coach who can assist you in this process.

This form can be downloaded as a PDF file at www.InnerGuidanceNetwork.org:
Spirits Onymous Campus: membership store: free stuff.

ACCOMPLISHMENTS PAGE

SPIRITS ONYMOUS WINTER SESSION 2008-2009

SUCCESS STORY
SPIRITS ONYMOUS WINTER SESSION 2008-2009

We would love to see your story!

For more information, go to www.InnerGuidanceNetwork.org, click on
"Spirits Onymous" and look for "Submit Your Success Story." Your story
may end up on the website and in next year's handbook.

PLANNER

From September 2007 to February 2009

DECEMBER 2007

Sun	Mon	Tue	Wed	Thu	Fri	Sat
						1
2	3	4	5	6	7	8
9	10	11	12	13	14	15
16	17	18	19	20	21	22
23	24	25	26	27	28	29
30	31					

USA Holidays and observances:

25: Christmas Day

Looking for a perfect holiday gift?

Order now copies of Spirits Onymous Handbook 2008 and/or The ClearView Conspiracy. Show your holiday spirit—give your friends and family a holiday gift that lifts their spirit and supports their quest for a meaningful and joyful life. Contact your local meeting host or order online: www.InnerGuidanceNetwork.org.

see page 6		A=	B=	C=	A	B	C
Sat	1						
Sun	2	Breathe					
Mon	3						
Tue	4						
Wed	5						
Thu	6						
Fr	7						
Sat	8						
Sun	9	Step 1: Align with your True Identity					
Mon	10						
Tue	11						
Wed	12						

Thu	13				
Fr	14				
Sat	15				
Sun	16	Step 2. Align with Stillness			
Mon	17				
Tue	18				
Wed	19				
Thu	20				
Fr	21				
Sat	22				
Sun	23	Step 3. Align with Now			
Mon	24				
Tue	25				
Wed	26				
Thu	27				
Fr	28				
Sat	29				
Sun	30	Step 4. Align with Your Original Intent			
Mon	31				

JANUARY 2008

Sun	Mon	Tue	Wed	Thu	Fri	Sat
		1	2	3	4	5
6	7	8	9	10	11	12
13	14	15	16	17	18	19
20	21	22	23	24	25	26
27	28	29	30	31		

USA Holidays and observances:

1: New Year's Day,

21: Martin Luther King Day

Notes:

see page 6		A=	B=	C=	A	B	C
Tue	1						
Wed	2						
Thu	3						
Fr	4						
Sat	5						
Sun	6	Step 5. Align with Your Inner Guide					
Mon	7						
Tue	8						
Wed	9						
Thu	10						
Fr	11						
Sat	12						

Sun	13	Step 6. Create a Goal Plan			
Mon	14				
Tue	15				
Wed	16				
Thu	17				
Fr	18				
Sat	19				
Sun	20	Step 7. Take Charge: The R-factor			
Mon	21				
Tue	22				
Wed	23				
Thu	24				
Fr	25				
Sat	26				
Sun	27	Step 8. Create a Mindfully: The Art of Mindful Creation			
Mon	28				
Tue	29				
Wed	30				
Thu	31				

FEBRUARY 2008

Sun	Mon	Tue	Wed	Thu	Fri	Sat
					1	2
3	4	5	6	7	8	9
10	11	12	13	14	15	16
17	18	19	20	21	22	23
24	25	26	27	28	29	

USA Holidays and observances:

14: Valentine's Day,

18: Washington's Birthday

Notes:

see page 6		A=	B=	C=	A	B	C
Fr	1						
Sat	2						
Sun	3	Step 9. Reach Enlightenment Now					
Mon	4						
Tue	5						
Wed	6						
Thu	7						
Fr	8						
Sat	9						
Sun	10	Step 10. Be a Mindful leader					

Mon	11				
Tue	12				
Wed	13				
Thu	14				
Fr	15				
Sat	16				
Sun	17	Step 11. Manifest Physical Resilience			
Mon	18				
Tue	19				
Wed	20				
Thu	21				
Fr	22				
Sat	23				
Sun	24	Step 12. Manifest a Sustainable World			
Mon	25				
Tue	26				
Wed	27				
Thu	28				
Fr	29				

MARCH 2008

Sun	Mon	Tue	Wed	Thu	Fri	Sat
						1
2	3	4	5	6	7	8
9	10	11	12	13	14	15
16	17	18	19	20	21	22
23	24	25	26	27	28	29
30	31					

USA Holidays and observances:

23: Easter Sunday

Notes:

see page 6		A=	B=	C=	A	B	C
Sat	1						
Sun	2	Breathe					
Mon	3						
Tue	4						
Wed	5						
Thu	6						
Fr	7						
Sat	8						
Sun	9	Step 1: Align with your True Identity					
Mon	10						
Tue	11						
Wed	12						

Thu	13				
Fr	14				
Sat	15				
Sun	16	Step 2. Align with Stillness			
Mon	17				
Tue	18				
Wed	19				
Thu	20				
Fr	21				
Sat	22				
Sun	23	Step 3. Align with Now			
Mon	24				
Tue	25				
Wed	26				
Thu	27				
Fr	28				
Sat	29				
Sun	30	Step 4. Align with Your Original Intent			
Mon	31				

APRIL 2008

Sun	Mon	Tue	Wed	Thu	Fri	Sat
		1	2	3	4	5
6	7	8	9	10	11	12
13	14	15	16	17	18	19
20	21	22	23	24	25	26
27	28	29	30			

Notes:

see page 6		A=	B=	C=	A	B	C
Tue	1						
Wed	2						
Thu	3						
Fr	4						
Sat	5						
Sun	6	Step 5. Align with Your Inner Guide					
Mon	7						
Tue	8						
Wed	9						
Thu	10						
Fr	11						

Sat	12				
Sun	13	Step 6. Create a Goal Plan			
Mon	14				
Tue	15				
Wed	16				
Thu	17				
Fr	18				
Sat	19				
Sun	20	Step 7. Take Charge: The R-factor			
Mon	21				
Tue	22				
Wed	23				
Thu	24				
Fr	25				
Sat	26				
Sun	27	Step 8. Create a Mindfully: The Art of Mindful Creation			
Mon	28				
Tue	29				
Wed	30				

MAY 2008

Sun	Mon	Tue	Wed	Thu	Fri	Sat
				1	2	3
4	5	6	7	8	9	10
11	12	13	14	15	16	17
18	19	20	21	22	23	24
25	26	27	28	29	30	31

USA Holidays and observances:

26: Memorial Day

Notes:

see page 6		A=	B=	C=	A	B	C
Thu	1						
Fr	2						
Sat	3						
Sun	4	Step 9. Reach Enlightenment Now					
Mon	5						
Tue	6						
Wed	7						
Thu	8						
Fr	9						
Sat	10						
Sun	11	Step 10. Be a Mindful leader					
Mon	12						

Tue	13				
Wed	14				
Thu	15				
Fr	16				
Sat	17				
Sun	18	Step 11. Manifest Physical Resilience			
Mon	19				
Tue	20				
Wed	21				
Thu	22				
Fr	23				
Sat	24				
Sun	25	Step 12. Manifest a Sustainable World			
Mon	26				
Tue	27				
Wed	28				
Thu	29				
Fr	30				
Sat	31				

JUNE 2008

Sun	Mon	Tue	Wed	Thu	Fri	Sat
1	2	3	4	5	6	7
8	9	10	11	12	13	14
15	16	17	18	19	20	21
22	23	24	25	26	27	28
29	30					

Notes:

see page 6	A=	B=	C=	A	B	C
Sun	1	Breathe				
Mon	2					
Tue	3					
Wed	4					
Thu	5					
Fr	6					
Sat	7					
Sun	8	Step 1: Align with your True Identity				
Mon	9					
Tue	10					
Wed	11					

Thu	12				
Fr	13				
Sat	14				
Sun	15	Step 2. Align with Stillness			
Mon	16				
Tue	17				
Wed	18				
Thu	19				
Fr	20				
Sat	21				
Sun	22	Step 3. Align with Now			
Mon	23				
Tue	24				
Wed	25				
Thu	26				
Fr	27				
Sat	28				
Sun	29	Step 4. Align with Your Original Intent			
Mon	30				

JULY 2008

Sun	Mon	Tue	Wed	Thu	Fri	Sat
		1	2	3	4	5
6	7	8	9	10	11	12
13	14	15	16	17	18	19
20	21	22	23	24	25	26
27	28	29	30	31		

USA Holidays and observances:

4: Independence Day

Notes:

see page 6	A=	B=	C=	A	B	C
Tue	1					
Wed	2					
Thu	3					
Fr	4					
Sat	5					
Sun	6	Step 5. Align with Your Inner Guide				
Mon	7					
Tue	8					
Wed	9					
Thu	10					
Fr	11					
Sat	12					

Sun	13	Step 6. Create a Goal Plan			
Mon	14				
Tue	15				
Wed	16				
Thu	17				
Fr	18				
Sat	19				
Sun	20	Step 7. Take Charge: The R-factor			
Mon	21				
Tue	22				
Wed	23				
Thu	24				
Fr	25				
Sat	26				
Sun	27	Step 8. Create a Mindfully: The Art of Mindful Creation			
Mon	28				
Tue	29				
Wed	30				
Thu	31				

AUGUST 2008

Sun	Mon	Tue	Wed	Thu	Fri	Sat
					1	2
3	4	5	6	7	8	9
10	11	12	13	14	15	16
17	18	19	20	21	22	23
24	25	26	27	28	29	30
31						

Notes:

see page 6		A=	B=	C=	A	B	C
Fr	1						
Sat	2						
Sun	3	Step 9. Reach Enlightenment Now					
Mon	4						
Tue	5						
Wed	6						
Thu	7						
Fr	8						
Sat	9						
Sun	10	Step 10. Be a Mindful leader					
Mon	11						
Tue	12						

Wed	13				
Thu	14				
Fr	15				
Sat	16				
Sun	17	Step 11. Manifest Physical Resilience			
Mon	18				
Tue	19				
Wed	20				
Thu	21				
Fr	22				
Sat	23				
Sun	24	Step 12. Manifest a Sustainable World			
Mon	25				
Tue	26				
Wed	27				
Thu	28				
Fr	29				
Sat	30				
Sun	31	Breathe			

SEPTEMBER 2008

Sun	Mon	Tue	Wed	Thu	Fri	Sat
		1	2	3	4	5	6
7	8	9	10	11	12	13
14	15	16	17	18	19	20
21	22	23	24	25	26	27
28	29	30				

USA Holidays and observances:

1: Labor Day

Notes:

see page 6		A=	B=	C=	A	B	C
Mon	1						
Tue	2						
Wed	3						
Thu	4						
Fr	5						
Sat	6						
Sun	7	Step 1: Align with your True Identity					
Mon	8						
Tue	9						
Wed	10						
Thu	11						

Fr	12				
Sat	13				
Sun	14	Step 2. Align with Stillness			
Mon	15				
Tue	16				
Wed	17				
Thu	18				
Fr	19				
Sat	20				
Sun	21	Step 3. Align with Now			
Mon	22				
Tue	23				
Wed	24				
Thu	25				
Fr	26				
Sat	27				
Sun	28	Step 4. Align with Your Original Intent			
Mon	29				
Tue	30				

OCTOBER 2008

Sun	Mon	Tue	Wed	Thu	Fri	Sat
			1	2	3	4
5	6	7	8	9	10	11
12	13	14	15	16	17	18
19	20	21	22	23	24	25
26	27	28	29	30	31	

USA Holidays and observances:

13: Columbus Day,

31: Halloween

Notes:

see page 6		A=	B=	C=	A	B	C
Wed	1						
Thu	2						
Fr	3						
Sat	4						
Sun	5	Step 5. Align with Your Inner Guide					
Mon	6						
Tue	7						
Wed	8						
Thu	9						
Fr	10						
Sat	11						
Sun	12	Step 6. Create a Goal Plan					

Mon	13				
Tue	14				
Wed	15				
Thu	16				
Fr	17				
Sat	18				
Sun	19	Step 7. Take Charge: The R-factor			
Mon	20				
Tue	21				
Wed	22				
Thu	23				
Fr	24				
Sat	25				
Sun	26	Step 8. Create a Mindfully: The Art of Mindful Creation			
Mon	27				
Tue	28				
Wed	29				
Thu	30				
Fr	31				

NOVEMBER 2008

Sun	Mon	Tue	Wed	Thu	Fri	Sat
						1
2	3	4	5	6	7	8
9	10	11	12	13	14	15
16	17	18	19	20	21	22
23	24	25	26	27	28	29
30						

USA Holidays and observances:

11: Veterans Day,

27: Thanksgiving Day

It's time for your "membership dues."

Instead of a membership fee, we ask you to purchase yearly three or more copies of the Spirits Onymous Handbook *(the 2009 edition is ready!) or* The ClearView Conspiracy *to give them as gifts. By doing this, you will invite family, friends and colleagues to let go of their attachment to drama and focus on the magnificence of life. You will be instrumental in helping them remember that indeed they are Spirit having a human experience. Contact your local meeting host or order online* www.InnerGuidanceNetwork.org.

see page 6		A=	B=	C=	A	B	C
Sat	1						
Sun	2	Step 9. Reach Enlightenment Now					
Mon	3						
Tue	4						
Wed	5						
Thu	6						
Fr	7						
Sat	8						
Sun	9	Step 10. Be a Mindful leader					
Mon	10						
Tue	11						

Wed	12				
Thu	13				
Fr	14				
Sat	15				
Sun	16	Step 11. Manifest Physical Resilience			
Mon	17				
Tue	18				
Wed	19				
Thu	20				
Fr	21				
Sat	22				
Sun	23	Step 12. Manifest a Sustainable World			
Mon	24				
Tue	25				
Wed	26				
Thu	27				
Fr	28				
Sat	29				
Sun	30	Breathe			

DECEMBER 2008

Sun	Mon	Tue	Wed	Thu	Fri	Sat
	1	2	3	4	5	6
7	8	9	10	11	12	13
14	15	16	17	18	19	20
21	22	23	24	25	26	27
28	29	30	31			

USA Holidays and observances:

25: Christmas Day

Looking for a perfect holiday gift?

Order now copies of <u>Spirits Onymous Handbook 2009</u> *and/or* <u>The ClearView Conspiracy</u>. *Show your holiday spirit—give your friends and family a holiday gift that lifts their spirit and supports their quest for a meaningful and joyful life. Contact your local meeting host or order online: <u>www.InnerGuidanceNetwork.org</u>.*

see page 6		A=	B=	C=	A	B	C
Mon	1						
Tue	2						
Wed	3						
Thu	4						
Fr	5						
Sat	6						
Sun	7	Step 1: Align with your True Identity					
Mon	8						
Tue	9						
Wed	10						
Thu	11						
Fr	12						

Sat	13				
Sun	14	Step 2. Align with Stillness			
Mon	15				
Tue	16				
Wed	17				
Thu	18				
Fr	19				
Sat	20				
Sun	21	Step 3. Align with Now			
Mon	22				
Tue	23				
Wed	24				
Thu	25				
Fr	26				
Sat	27				
Sun	28	Step 4. Align with Your Original Intent			
Mon	29				
Tue	30				
Wed	31				

JANUARY 2009

Sun	Mon	Tue	Wed	Thu	Fri	Sat
				1	2	3
4	5	6	7	8	9	10
11	12	13	14	15	16	17
18	19	20	21	22	23	24
25	26	27	28	29	30	31

USA Holidays and observances:

1: New Year's Day,

19: Martin Luther King Day

Notes:

see page 6		A=	B=	C=	A	B	C
Thu	1						
Fr	2						
Sat	3						
Sun	4	Step 5. Align with Your Inner Guide					
Mon	5						
Tue	6						
Wed	7						
Thu	8						
Fr	9						
Sat	10						
Sun	11	Step 6. Create a Goal Plan					
Mon	12						

Tue	13				
Wed	14				
Thu	15				
Fr	16				
Sat	17				
Sun	18	Step 7. Take Charge: The R-factor			
Mon	19				
Tue	20				
Wed	21				
Thu	22				
Fr	23				
Sat	24				
Sun	25	Step 8. Create a Mindfully: The Art of Mindful Creation			
Mon	26				
Tue	27				
Wed	28				
Thu	29				
Fr	30				
Sat	31				

FEBRUARY 2009

Sun	Mon	Tue	Wed	Thu	Fri	Sat
1	2	3	4	5	6	7
8	9	10	11	12	13	14
15	16	17	18	19	20	21
22	23	24	25	26	27	28

USA Holidays and observances:

14: Valentine's Day,

16: Washington's Birthday

Notes:

see page 6		A=	B=	C=	A	B	C
Sun	1	Step 9. Reach Enlightenment Now					
Mon	2						
Tue	3						
Wed	4						
Thu	5						
Fr	6						
Sat	7						
Sun	8	Step 10. Be a Mindful leader					
Mon	9						
Tue	10						

Adrianus – The InnerGuidance Network

Wed	11				
Thu	12				
Fr	13				
Sat	14				
Sun	15	Step 11. Manifest Physical Resilience			
Mon	16				
Tue	17				
Wed	18				
Thu	19				
Fr	20				
Sat	21				
Sun	22	Step 12. Manifest a Sustainable World			
Mon	23				
Tue	24				
Wed	25				
Thu	26				
Fr	27				
Sat	28				

2007

January 2007

Su	Mo	Tu	We	Th	Fr	Sa
	1	2	3	4	5	6
7	8	9	10	11	12	13
14	15	16	17	18	19	20
21	22	23	24	25	26	27
28	29	30	31			

February 2007

Su	Mo	Tu	We	Th	Fr	Sa
				1	2	3
4	5	6	7	8	9	10
11	12	13	14	15	16	17
18	19	20	21	22	23	24
25	26	27	28			

March 2007

Su	Mo	Tu	We	Th	Fr	Sa
				1	2	3
4	5	6	7	8	9	10
11	12	13	14	15	16	17
18	19	20	21	22	23	24
25	26	27	28	29	30	31

April 2007

Su	Mo	Tu	We	Th	Fr	Sa
1	2	3	4	5	6	7
8	9	10	11	12	13	14
15	16	17	18	19	20	21
22	23	24	25	26	27	28
29	30					

May 2007

Su	Mo	Tu	We	Th	Fr	Sa
		1	2	3	4	5
6	7	8	9	10	11	12
13	14	15	16	17	18	19
20	21	22	23	24	25	26
27	28	29	30	31		

June 2007

Su	Mo	Tu	We	Th	Fr	Sa
					1	2
3	4	5	6	7	8	9
10	11	12	13	14	15	16
17	18	19	20	21	22	23
24	25	26	27	28	29	30

July 2007

Su	Mo	Tu	We	Th	Fr	Sa
1	2	3	4	5	6	7
8	9	10	11	12	13	14
15	16	17	18	19	20	21
22	23	24	25	26	27	28
29	30	31				

August 2007

Su	Mo	Tu	We	Th	Fr	Sa
			1	2	3	4
5	6	7	8	9	10	11
12	13	14	15	16	17	18
19	20	21	22	23	24	25
26	27	28	29	30	31	

September 2007

Su	Mo	Tu	We	Th	Fr	Sa
						1
2	3	4	5	6	7	8
9	10	11	12	13	14	15
16	17	18	19	20	21	22
23	24	25	26	27	28	29
30						

October 2007

Su	Mo	Tu	We	Th	Fr	Sa
	1	2	3	4	5	6
7	8	9	10	11	12	13
14	15	16	17	18	19	20
21	22	23	24	25	26	27
28	29	30	31			

November 2007

Su	Mo	Tu	We	Th	Fr	Sa
				1	2	3
4	5	6	7	8	9	10
11	12	13	14	15	16	17
18	19	20	21	22	23	24
25	26	27	28	29	30	

December 2007

Su	Mo	Tu	We	Th	Fr	Sa
						1
2	3	4	5	6	7	8
9	10	11	12	13	14	15
16	17	18	19	20	21	22
23	24	25	26	27	28	29
30	31					

2008

January 2008

Su	Mo	Tu	We	Th	Fr	Sa
		1	2	3	4	5
6	7	8	9	10	11	12
13	14	15	16	17	18	19
20	21	22	23	24	25	26
27	28	29	30	31		

February 2008

Su	Mo	Tu	We	Th	Fr	Sa
					1	2
3	4	5	6	7	8	9
10	11	12	13	14	15	16
17	18	19	20	21	22	23
24	25	26	27	28	29	

March 2008

Su	Mo	Tu	We	Th	Fr	Sa
						1
2	3	4	5	6	7	8
9	10	11	12	13	14	15
16	17	18	19	20	21	22
23	24	25	26	27	28	29
30	31					

April 2008

Su	Mo	Tu	We	Th	Fr	Sa
		1	2	3	4	5
6	7	8	9	10	11	12
13	14	15	16	17	18	19
20	21	22	23	24	25	26
27	28	29	30			

May 2008

Su	Mo	Tu	We	Th	Fr	Sa
				1	2	3
4	5	6	7	8	9	10
11	12	13	14	15	16	17
18	19	20	21	22	23	24
25	26	27	28	29	30	31

June 2008

Su	Mo	Tu	We	Th	Fr	Sa
1	2	3	4	5	6	7
8	9	10	11	12	13	14
15	16	17	18	19	20	21
22	23	24	25	26	27	28
29	30					

July 2008

Su	Mo	Tu	We	Th	Fr	Sa
		1	2	3	4	5
6	7	8	9	10	11	12
13	14	15	16	17	18	19
20	21	22	23	24	25	26
27	28	29	30	31		

August 2008

Su	Mo	Tu	We	Th	Fr	Sa
					1	2
3	4	5	6	7	8	9
10	11	12	13	14	15	16
17	18	19	20	21	22	23
24	25	26	27	28	29	30
31						

September 2008

Su	Mo	Tu	We	Th	Fr	Sa
	1	2	3	4	5	6
7	8	9	10	11	12	13
14	15	16	17	18	19	20
21	22	23	24	25	26	27
28	29	30				

October 2008

Su	Mo	Tu	We	Th	Fr	Sa
			1	2	3	4
5	6	7	8	9	10	11
12	13	14	15	16	17	18
19	20	21	22	23	24	25
26	27	28	29	30	31	

November 2008

Su	Mo	Tu	We	Th	Fr	Sa
						1
2	3	4	5	6	7	8
9	10	11	12	13	14	15
16	17	18	19	20	21	22
23	24	25	26	27	28	29
30						

December 2008

Su	Mo	Tu	We	Th	Fr	Sa
	1	2	3	4	5	6
7	8	9	10	11	12	13
14	15	16	17	18	19	20
21	22	23	24	25	26	27
28	29	30	31			

2009

January 2009

Su	Mo	Tu	We	Th	Fr	Sa
				1	2	3
4	5	6	7	8	9	10
11	12	13	14	15	16	17
18	19	20	21	22	23	24
25	26	27	28	29	30	31

February 2009

Su	Mo	Tu	We	Th	Fr	Sa
1	2	3	4	5	6	7
8	9	10	11	12	13	14
15	16	17	18	19	20	21
22	23	24	25	26	27	28

March 2009

Su	Mo	Tu	We	Th	Fr	Sa
1	2	3	4	5	6	7
8	9	10	11	12	13	14
15	16	17	18	19	20	21
22	23	24	25	26	27	28
29	30	31				

April 2009

Su	Mo	Tu	We	Th	Fr	Sa
			1	2	3	4
5	6	7	8	9	10	11
12	13	14	15	16	17	18
19	20	21	22	23	24	25
26	27	28	29	30		

May 2009

Su	Mo	Tu	We	Th	Fr	Sa
					1	2
3	4	5	6	7	8	9
10	11	12	13	14	15	16
17	18	19	20	21	22	23
24	25	26	27	28	29	30
31						

June 2009

Su	Mo	Tu	We	Th	Fr	Sa
	1	2	3	4	5	6
7	8	9	10	11	12	13
14	15	16	17	18	19	20
21	22	23	24	25	26	27
28	29	30				

July 2009

Su	Mo	Tu	We	Th	Fr	Sa
			1	2	3	4
5	6	7	8	9	10	11
12	13	14	15	16	17	18
19	20	21	22	23	24	25
26	27	28	29	30	31	

August 2009

Su	Mo	Tu	We	Th	Fr	Sa
						1
2	3	4	5	6	7	8
9	10	11	12	13	14	15
16	17	18	19	20	21	22
23	24	25	26	27	28	29
30	31					

September 2009

Su	Mo	Tu	We	Th	Fr	Sa
		1	2	3	4	5
6	7	8	9	10	11	12
13	14	15	16	17	18	19
20	21	22	23	24	25	26
27	28	29	30			

October 2009

Su	Mo	Tu	We	Th	Fr	Sa
				1	2	3
4	5	6	7	8	9	10
11	12	13	14	15	16	17
18	19	20	21	22	23	24
25	26	27	28	29	30	31

November 2009

Su	Mo	Tu	We	Th	Fr	Sa
1	2	3	4	5	6	7
8	9	10	11	12	13	14
15	16	17	18	19	20	21
22	23	24	25	26	27	28
29	30					

December 2009

Su	Mo	Tu	We	Th	Fr	Sa
		1	2	3	4	5
6	7	8	9	10	11	12
13	14	15	16	17	18	19
20	21	22	23	24	25	26
27	28	29	30	31		

Adrianus – The InnerGuidance Network

SHOW CASE

I would like to express my gratitude to three amazing women: Patricia Omoqui, Karen Drucker and Zulma Alvarez.

Patricia Omoqui, an amazingly gifted and poetic spirit, contributed fourteen beautiful poems to this book. That's right; we have one more treasure in store: next page!

Karen Drucker has been uplifting my spirits for several years. Her music is mood and mind transforming and I feel honored that I found Karen willing to contribute to the meditations. Her "Blessing to the World" is such a wonderful opening.

Zulma Alvarez is a passionate and warm soul who supported me day-by-day during the production of this book. She is an amazingly talented professional life coach who assists me in staying focused. She is an even greater life partner. No bias!

Awareness is

Growing all around you
You can see this
In the miraculous openings of
The people in your lives

See that people are beginning
To smile more
To open their hearts
To trust their fellow humans
To know that the world can make a great shift
A great leap into new consciousness

Be prepared, for a Shift is coming

You will enjoy the shift
You are ready to lead the way
Be at the front of the pack
Speak to the crowds of people
Who are ready to hear

They are open to your words
Spirit will speak through you
Just open to opportunities to speak
Spirit will send many people to you

Follow inner guidance; listen to your inner voice

Patricia Omoqui

Patricia is a uniquely inspiring speaker, author, poet and life coach. As a speaker, Patricia delivers her message with passion igniting the best in individuals and organizations, empowering all to understand and step into their own true power and potential. Some topics that Patricia speaks on are:

- Keys to Becoming an Exceptional Mentor

- Harness Your Power: Achieve Everything You Desire in Life

- Control Your Thoughts, Control Your Life

- Live in the Now: Fully Access Your Potential

Patricia is an internationally recognized writer. Her inspirational articles and poetic meditations have inspired people around the world. Her daily e-mail list, *Food For Thought*, has been described by readers as an "e-mail jewel", "a mental mini-spa" and a "comforting way to start the day".

As a life coach, Patricia works with individuals and groups that are ready to move quickly towards change in order to reach their dreams and achieve their full potential in life.

For more information on the products and services that Patricia Omoqui can offer to you or your organization, please visit her on the web at www.patriciaomoqui.com or call her at 610-616-4505.

Blessing to the World

You are the heart
You are the hands
You are the voice of Spirit on Earth
And who you are
And all you do
Is a blessing to the world.

We are the heart
We are the hands
We are the voice of Spirit on Earth
And who we are
And all we do
Is a blessing to the world.

I am the heart
I am the hands
I am the voice of Spirit on Earth
And I am
And all I do
Is a blessing to the world.

Words: Karen Drucker and Rev. David Bruner
Music: Karen Drucker

Karen Drucker

Karen has recorded 11 albums of her original inspirational music and has won numerous awards for her volunteer work for performing and producing shows for organizations in need. She has been a professional comedienne, led her own band for corporate events, and has been a performer and spokeswoman for "Bread and Roses" (performing in convalescent hospitals, prisons, children's hospitals, etc). She started her own organization "Artists for a Cause" to raise awareness and funds for organizations in need by producing concerts featuring local entertainers.

She has been the music director for three different Religious Science churches; she sings, speaks and leads workshops at women's retreats, mind-body and health conferences and various churches around the country and performs music for ministers, workshop facilitators, including Joan Borysenko, SARK, and Oriah Mountain Dreamer.

- She was awarded an Honorary Doctorate in music from the United Church of Religious Science.

- She swam the English Channel with five other women becoming the first American women's relay team to make a successful crossing.

- She rode her bike from San Francisco to Los Angeles in the AIDS ride.

- She walked from Santa Barbara to Malibu in the Avon breast cancer walk.

- She had her own TV show when she was 21.

- But her most impressive achievement was winning the international Tarzan calling contest when she was 13.

She loves making music, making a difference and touching hearts …

To learn more and order CDs: www.karendrucker.com

Excerpts from Zulma's "I AM CONNECTED" weekly E-zine

Have you been listening to the call of your destiny? Are you imagining with a childlike, playful, curiosity? I wonder if our destiny is to fully embrace the belief that we are Divine creators.

—

Since we are Spiritual beings having a human experience, I believe, we are invited to feel our feelings and heal the victim aspect of ourselves. In doing so, we connect with our Inner Authority and live joyfully in the present moment.

—

Unconscious beliefs from our childhood are slippery little fellows. They can dictate the decisions we make, our feelings about ourselves, and how we perceive the world.

It appears that our Spirit draws to us the people who will mirror our unconscious beliefs. These beliefs may have been formed for protection. By becoming conscious of the pattern, we then can reconnect with our true essence...Spirit.

May you have many opportunities to acknowledge that you are an expression of Spirit and that all is well, no matter how life appears to your ego.

—

When I AM connected to my spiritual source, I can easily offer others and myself unconditional love. Hence, when I am challenged in loving others and myself, it is a clue that I have disconnected from Spirit.

When I am critical, blaming, or fearful, I notice that I move away from my True Nature. By recognizing my emotional discomfort, I can then choose to reconnect with my True Self, which is loving, accepting and allowing.

The power is you and the moment is now,

Zulma

Zulma I. Alvarez

Zulma is a Certified Life Coach. She partners with exceptional professionals to clarify their mission and live authentically. Zulma received her training and certification from the Coach Training Alliance, which is accredited by the International Coaching Federation.

Her areas of expertise are spirituality, personal development and mastering change. She incorporates these skills in individual coaching sessions and in workshops.

Zulma has worked for more than thirty years in various positions in corporate, education, retail and alternative healthcare.

She is the past Vice President of the Colonial Quilters Guild and a certified Reiki Master. As a life-long resident of Bethlehem, Pennsylvania, Zulma incorporates the "I AM" philosophy with support from her family, friends, meditation, quilting and gardening.

She invites you to manifest your next step with an experiential and eclectic approach. Her intention is to experience and model mindfulness and to create an authentic and meaningful life.

For more information and a complimentary 30-minute session, go to her website: www.InnerAuthorityMindfulness.com.

"I appreciate Zulma's innate ability to listen especially to what I am not saying. She asks powerful questions, which assist me in attaining focus and supports me in formalizing a plan of action that is clear and doable. Zulma is enthusiastic, honest and direct in her feedback to me. At the end of the session, I feel good about my direction and confident in how to accomplish my next goal."

- Julie D., St. Louis, MO

***The ClearView Conspiracy* is a fast-paced spiritual adventure that takes you on a thought-provoking quest deep into your own soul.**

John Milford—*an investigative journalist from Pennsylvania*—receives a phone call from a stranger, begging for help, "They are using me as a human guinea pig." While dodging attacks on his life, John hounds a trail of a large pharmaceutical company that leads into the Ecuadorian jungle and to a secret underground control center in Germany.

The more John delves into the evidence of crime, the more he uncovers the astonishing truth about himself and the existence of mankind. The ClearView Conspiracy takes you on a suspenseful journey that casts a mind-altering view on life, and reveals the cosmic significance of every conflict, every moment, every breath.

His Holiness The Dalai Lama, Gurumayi Chidvilasananda, Dan Millman, Pir Zia Inayat Khan, The Venerable Khandro Rinpoche, and Andrew Harvey are characters in the book and unveil—*in their own words*—the absolute truth of who we are.

"Adrianus has written a fascinating and imaginative tale of intrigue as a creative means of conveying significant spiritual concepts. It's also a darn good read and a great way to spend a weekend!"
  - Terri B. Trigiani

"What powerful images and characters you have created! You pack such descriptions and such vivid imagery into a few paragraphs. This story is one that educates and informs -- as well as creates suspense."
  - Nancy Miller

"I enjoyed the book very much. I found the story and style reminiscent of The Celestine Prophecy."
  - Brian Shoemaker

"Thank you for this wonderful book. I read it in one afternoon! I just couldn't put it down!"
  - Cas Styrcula

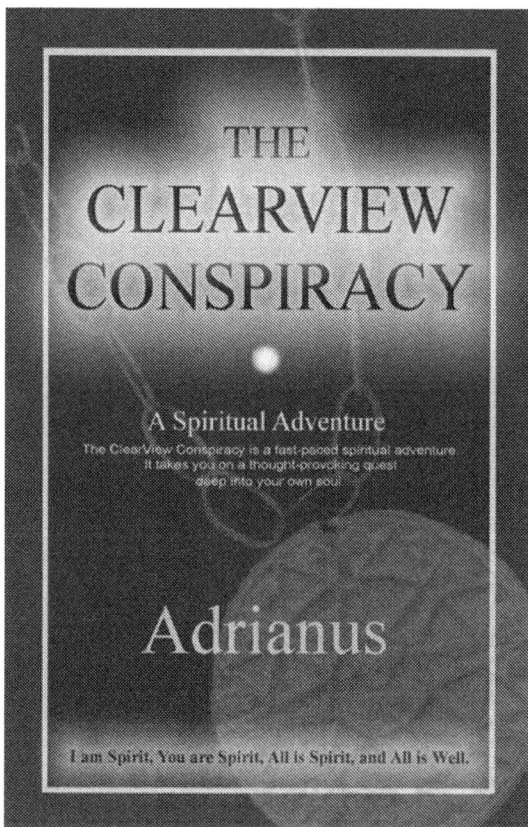

THE
CLEARVIEW
CONSPIRACY

A Spiritual Adventure
The ClearView Conspiracy is a fast-paced spiritual adventure.
It takes you on a thought-provoking quest
deep into your own soul.

Adrianus

I am Spirit, You are Spirit, All is Spirit, and All is Well.

www.ClearViewConspiracy.com

"The ClearView Conspiracy hooks the reader right from the start by creating that sense of 'what's going to happen next,' which spurs the reader forward from chapter to chapter."
  - Laurie Stauffer

"The ClearView Conspiracy gave me a jump-start to a place within which I really understand that we are all Spirits here to do spiritual work. Layers of forgetting were allowed to drop away, and I find such joy in viewing myself and others in this wonderful light."
  - Barbara Heffel

"I found myself falling into childhood behavior of "gorge reading," and needed to stop myself, walk away and commit to slowing the pace. I am very intrigued."
  - Melissa Hightower